A. B Morrison

Spiritualism and Necromancy

A. B Morrison

Spiritualism and Necromancy

ISBN/EAN: 9783337042233

Printed in Europe, USA, Canada, Australia, Japan

Cover: Foto ©Lupo / pixelio.de

More available books at **www.hansebooks.com**

Spiritualism

AND

Necromancy.

BY

REV. A. B. MORRISON,
Of the Southern Illinois Conference.

———◆———

CINCINNATI:
HITCHCOCK AND WALDEN.
NEW YORK:
NELSON AND PHILLIPS.
1873.

Entered, according to Act of Congress, in the year 1873,

BY HITCHCOCK & WALDEN,

In the Office of the Librarian of Congress, at Washington.

PREFACE.

AFTER the publication of our two sermons, or lectures, on Spiritualism and Necromancy, our mind turned naturally to a further investigation of the claims of spiritualism; and as we studied the subject deeper and closer, we determined to write out our discoveries and deductions, for our own use. This we have done in the form of lectures, something after the manner of sermonizing; for such is our habit of thought.

The production has been so interesting to us, and our former publication having received such favor, we have been encouraged to give this also to the public; being impelled to do so with strong hope of doing some good, by arresting the tide of the ruinous heresy of spiritualism. We are aware that we shall meet the anathemas of those who have already fallen into this snare of the devil; but we hope to win back, to God and reason, honest souls who have been tempted to tamper with this serpent of sin.

In our fifth and seventh lectures we look, too, for opposition from "the orthodox;" but, after careful study, aided by such helps as we could command, we have deliberately and solidly concluded that "the Man of Sin" is not the "Old Man at Rome." We are willing to admit that he is a sinner, and that he is possessed of the spirit of Antichrist; but we can not determine, by Bible or history, that he is the Antichrist of prophecy. Our seventh lecture, on the Spirit of Inquiry, or Office and Use of Philosophy, is largely extracted from a review we wrote, a year ago, of Dr. Cocker's "Greek Philosophy;" and, as it had never been given to the public, and seemed to us to meet and express a felt want of our nature, so evidently manifest in the restless instability of man away from his God, we determined to insert it in this publication. Having prepared it in a little different form for ministerial criticism, we submit it to the laity without fear, trusting that it will do good, by showing in easy thought to the common reader that man, estranged from God by sin, is ever restless and unsatisfied until he be restored to the Father, through the merit of the Son. The other chapters treat directly of Spiritualism, with all its diabolism and hatefulness.

We have in crude outline another work, showing the true medium of spirit-communication, which may or may not go to the public. Future circumstances shall determine.

A. B. M.

CONTENTS.

		PAGE.
I.	Spiritualism and Necromancy,	9
II.	Spiritualism an Agency of Satan,	36
III.	Spiritualism and Demonology,	62
IV.	Spiritualism an Agency of Satan,	83
V.	Spiritualism and Antichrist,	98
VI.	Deception of Spiritualism,	112
VII.	The Spirit of Inquiry in Man,	126
VIII.	A Word to Spiritualists,	146
IX.	Bible Spiritualism,	166
X.	Spiritualism a Lover of Darkness,	186

INTRODUCTION.

FROM its earliest history, Methodism has carried on a vigorous warfare in defense of spiritual Christianity. It has been not only a stirring appeal and invitation of mercy to sinners, but also a bold note of warning to souls who have fallen into the snares of false religion. Our fathers were conspicuous for their boldness and readiness in attacking vagaries of unbelief, and every form of false doctrine. In this country, the itinerant ministry has pursued the same methods. But the concessions that our Government makes to religious liberty and freedom of speech and worship, offer facilities for the propagation of false religion, of which the spirit of evil has been alert to take advantage.

The author of this little volume has chosen to appear in print, not to achieve the notoriety of authorship, but to carry the practical results of his pastorate into a wider field. In the course of his regular duties, the delusion known as spiritualism, through the advocacy of one who had formerly been a Methodist preacher, produced bewilderment and perplexity in the minds of some over whom he had spiritual care. He wisely entered the lists in defense of the truth as it is in Christ. The success of his public effort, embodied in two sermons, called for their publication as desirable and profitable to his Church; and out of these has grown this larger essay.

Spiritualism has had a wonderful growth in the United States in the twenty-five years since the Misses Fox, of New York State, first gained the public attention. By bold assertions and shrewd practices, it has bewildered and entrapped some honest people whose curiosity was excited, and they have received spiritual harm. For modern spiritualism, as a system of religious thought and faith, is identical in origin and analogous in spirit and practice to that of demonology, which Inspiration has described as the doctrine of devils. It has borne no good fruit. . The classes it attracts by its teachings, and whose lives it fails to reform, are a standing proof of its worthlessness as a religious system. It has swept many into the most vicious forms of immorality and wickedness. It has added nothing to our knowledge of this life or of the world to come.

This pernicious belief has but to be examined and judged by the light of the Sacred Scriptures, the teaching of history, and in its unvarying tendency to pervert the moral life of its disciples, to be seen in its true character. This is the aim of the author of this volume. He defines and sets forth its proper character and constant tendencies, comparing it with the spiritualism taught in the Word of God. We commend it to all who are seeking to know the truth. We are confident that its perusal will prove a benefit to those whose minds are in doubt and need such light as its pages offer. A knowledge of its contents will prepare any one to ward off the subtleties of the deceiver of souls, and establish the conviction that spiritualism is the most dangerous form of unbelief with which Christianity has now to contend.

BENJ. ST. JAMES FRY.

ST. LOUIS, *June* 6, 1873.

Spiritualism and Necromancy.

I.

SPIRITUALISM AND NECROMANCY.

"There shall not be found among you any one that maketh his son or his daughter to pass through the fire, or that useth divination, or an observer of times, or an enchanter, or a witch, or a charmer, or a consulter with familiar spirits, or a wizard, or a necromancer. For all that do these things are an abomination unto the Lord: and because of these abominations the Lord thy God doth drive them out before thee."—DEUT. XVIII, 10-12.

SINCE the unfortunate fall of our race, every recorded act of man has been in clear demonstration of the Bible doctrine of our alienation from God and from righteousness. And it has ever been the studied policy of Satan, that old seducer, so to blind the eyes of men as to keep them in ignorance of God. A thousand years ago, this was no difficult task; but, with Bible-houses and a free press, Satan must bestir himself, or the light of the ages must fall on and illuminate the eye of reason in the masses of men. So, the very Pandora's box of hell has, within a hundred years, been opened out to earth's inhabitants, for the tangling of their feet and the snaring of their souls; and every-where men are seeking to hew out to themselves new cisterns, in the vain hope of finding in some one of them the elixir of the soul's life.

It is not a new weapon of war that Satan uses, when he throws the blinding cloud of doubt over the mental vision of man—bringing in strong delusions, trusting that men may believe a lie that they may be damned; for he has been all too successful in the ruin of souls with this weapon to abandon it now. Nor does he hesitate in using things real to induce men to believe things unreal; nor the contrary, the use of things unreal to induce men to believe things real. All this to delude men, and keep out, or shut out, the light of the Gospel, and the true service that God requires. Anciently, he habitually used the art of the magician and soothsayer, sorcery and divination; to-day, he uses the arts and sciences, perverting them. He seizes the Bible doctrine of spirit communication, abusing and perverting it into a lie. The warfare is the same; the weapons are nearly identical. Their appliance only is different; then he used magic, now he uses spirit. We notice:

1. Ancient necromancy and modern spiritualism are identical. By the term necromancy, we mean now to include the theory that men on the earth are able, by spirit alliance, to converse with the spirits of the dead, and thereby get a knowledge of the spirit-world; for a necromancer is properly one who pretends to foretell future events by holding converse with departed spirits, and one who uses sorcery and enchantments.

Young says, "A necromancer is a trickster." Gregory says, "Conjuration, or the black art." *Necronite* is, in the Greek, "*fœtid;*" while *necropolis* is the city of the dead, with whom the ancient necromancer claimed to be on familiar terms, and with whom they claimed to converse at pleasure; and by such conversation they claimed to know future events. For this purpose they used divination, of which there were many sorts, as is implied in the original expression here, "*Kasem, Kasamim*"—seeking to know, by unlawful arts and practices, things secret or to come. They were very superstitious; and, by closely observing the planets and the weather, they pronounced one day lucky and another unlucky. By such means they obtained the mastery of the superstitious minds of the masses, who had no means of refuting them; for they were also jugglers, causing things by some secret art to assume a false appearance, and thus would practice illusions on the people's fancy, and deceive by the slight of hand. These pretenders were wont to use superstitious words in their incantations; and, by observing the waters, looking through smoke, and other foolish ceremonies, they conjectured the destiny of the spirit. They used witchcraft, or were admitted to be in league and covenant with the devil, by whose help they deluded the people's senses, etc., through evil arts. The word is "*nachash*," where it is in the plural; it is *sorcerer*, who is one who transforms natural things so as to deceive the eye, not only deceiving, but getting possession of the will-power of the deceived.

The word is sometimes translated soothsayer—sooth and say; for they pretend to know and tell the events of life and future things. And because of this, then secret, power of mesmerism—for it was nothing else—they were called charmers; for, at this juncture, the devotee would, by means of ventriloquism, make the astonished subjects believe that they were in familiar conversation with the spirits of the dead. Hence Moses, in the text, calls them "consulters with familiar spirits." The original word is "*Shoel Ob*," and is, literally, "one who speaks out of his belly," and inquires of Ob, which means a bottle, and was the name given by the Hebrews to the spirit, and was aptly applied to those deceivers; for, during the process of their divinations, or *seance* (sa-ance), they distended their bodies violently, as a leather bottle full of new wine. Galen says, "Such persons violently distend their bodies like leather bottles full of wine, ready to burst, and speak as if their voice was sent from their bellies." Whoever has witnessed the art and heard the words of the professional juggler will comprehend this, and also see that such shabby tricks are not yet extinct; but, with the practice of such arts, the heathen nations of the land which Israel was to occupy and possess, were able to palm themselves off as wizards and necromancers; for these terms were not then offensive. The one signified "a knowing man;" the other, "a consulter of the dead." Their manner of doing so was to lie down in some dark place in the night, usually on or at the grave of him whose spirit they would consult, and then, after muttering strange and unintelligible words, in low, solemn, guttural sounds, would pretend to have communion with the spirit, and would sometimes claim to have seen the spirit. Such, then, is a brief outline of ancient necromancy.

My proposition identifies modern spiritualism with it; and, if the identity be maintained, we need but refer to the terrible maledictions of God upon the one, to be conscious of his disapprobation of the other.

Diviner, observer of times, enchanter, witch a consulter with familiar spirits, a wizard, and a necromancer, signified the same characters, in the performance of their several practices; as the term architect signifies builder, who may be laying the foundation, or mounting the turret. So, for convenience, we may use the general term "necromancy," and notice its work, as compared with spiritualism.

The necromancer pretended to know, by means of spirit communication, future events. Webster says, "By magic, enchantment, witchcraft, and divination, by the assistance of evil spirits;" that is, as we understand him, by help of the devil. Now, is there any thing in spiritualism like this practice?

A medical medium, or clairvoyant, in Boston, on Washington Street, advertises after this manner:

"MAGNETIC TREATMENT!
BUSINESS MEDIUM!
TURKISH LOVE POWDERS! SOMETHING NEW!
Ladies in trouble! Finding lost property," etc.;

and all this she pretends to carry on by aid of the spirits of the ancients, for the moderate

SPIRITUALISM AND NECROMANCY.

sum of two dollars! not including medicines, some particular kinds of which are exorbitantly high.

It is estimated that the fifty medical mediums in Boston realize an aggregate income of six hundred thousand dollars, for soothsaying the fortunes of the thousands who go to their *seances* daily; and it is worthy of note, that nearly all mediums who have the shrewdness to do so, resort to the medical trick for gain, in money and lust. But we notice:

The necromancer was a consulter with familiar spirits; that is, they pretended to talk with the spirits of the dead. Webster says, "Familiar spirit, a demon or evil spirit, supposed to attend a call."

By this means, the damsel spoken of in the sixteenth chapter of the Acts of the Apostles "brought great gain to her masters;" and, like the modern follower of the Fates, they were quite angry when the circle was broken, and the power of the medium blasted by the name of the Lord Jesus. Sorcery was a recognized practice in the days of the apostles, and Simon Magus supposed it was by this means the Holy Ghost was given. But, are there any such practices in spiritualism? Let us see. Here is an abstract from the *Boston Daily News*, July 25, 1872:

"Mrs. Harding, a noted medium of Boston, gets two dollars for getting dead relatives to come and converse with their living friends. Hundreds visit her daily. To get a 'setting,' you must send in your application several days in advance, otherwise your desire to converse with a relative will be denied. This woman was in poverty five years ago, when she hit upon the happy art of clairvoyance, or spiritualism; now, her income is said to be eighty dollars per day."

"By her soothsaying her masters had great gain" (Acts xvi); and, by Mrs. Harding's spiritualism, she has, in five years, sprung from poverty to a princely fortune. The same paper says her house, at No. 4 Concord Square, cost her twenty thousand dollars, and is furnished at an expense of eight thousand dollars, while her bank account is as creditable as the largest wholesale houses in the city. In a business sense, with her, spiritualism is no "humbug."

But the necromancer of Moses' day was also a wizard. In plain English, a wizard is a conjurer, or one who resorts to tricks and sleight of hand, for the purpose of causing imaginary things to seem true, making the unreal to appear real, the false to seem true, etc.

Dr. Waterland, an author of some note, says it properly means one who consulted the dead, and he describes their manner of doing so: "They, the 'wizards,' went to the grave of the dead in the night, stretched themselves upon them, and muttered as from the belly, or in ventriloquism." To this Isaiah is thought to refer, in the nineteenth verse of the eighth chapter. Hear the quotation: "And when they shall say unto you, Seek unto them that have familiar spirits, and unto wizards that peep and mutter: should not a people seek unto their God?" Then Isaiah challenges thus: "To the law and to the testimony: if they speak not according to this word, it is because there is no light in them."

Now, are there any such "peepings" and mutterings in spiritualism? Let us see; and we will not, dare not now, descend to the low, sluttish *seance* of home manufacture, where the lowest order of ignorant men and women cherish the baser passions, whose spawn is treachery and free-loveism, and the consequent concomitant, violation of the conjugal vow; but we prefer giving its fairest lights.

An unmarried and, we are told, eloquent divine, of Alton City, determined, some months ago, to "leave his own little corner of the Lord's vineyard to grow up in weeds," and visit the great Mecca of spiritual manifestation, which "Mecca" is an obscure village in the State of New York, called Moravia; and the result of his visit is in print, and so becomes public property. We quote only a few of the leading features of the article; for, as it appeared in the *St. Louis Democrat*, July 10th, most of you have read it.

He says: "Kind reader, imagine yourself in a country house," etc.; "a circle of seven is formed, hands are joined, the medium faces us." "The light is excluded; but a lamp is burning." "The only door is bolted;" "now the lamp is extinguished—all is dark." Suddenly, "the piano begins to play. Nothing is touching the keys; but the playing goes on." "Now, voices, seemingly above us, join in the song with great power and sweetness." The author does not tell us whether he learned the tune or not, nor the name of the song. We shall in a moment speak of optical illusion.

But, just now, we have something that reminds us of the wizards that "peeped"—the evidence of sound. A little study of the habits of the ancient necromancer will fully explain this sound, or those "peepings." They—while in the dark—muttered, murmuring words that seemed to be the voice of another. So Mrs. Andrews—who was our author's medium—with a knowledge of mesmerism and ventriloquism, while in the dark, spake and sang, as did the wizards of Moses' day. But now, while the mind is beclouded, and every nerve of the soul is on the stretch, it is a fitting time for yet other display of the spirits.

Accordingly, "mysterious lights began to dance in circles about the room;" which was doubtless but an optical illusion, aided by the magic-lantern in the hand of Mrs. Andrews, who was just then behind the "velvet curtain of the cabinet." And now, while the mind is so entranced, "soft voices whisper startling things in our ears"—whether those "startling things" were of earth or of heaven the narrator does not tell us—but "delicate hands thrill us with gentle and affectionate touches," and "tender lips kissed mine." No marvel that he was speechless. We have read, in 1 Samuel xxviii, 7 (it was after Saul had got tired serving Israel's God, and God had forsaken him), he said to his servants, "Seek me a woman that hath a familiar spirit." At Endor, he found just such a woman, and her performances were so overpowering that Saul fell down in a swoon.

But our author was now sufficiently wrought up to get nearer the medium, which he did, even shutting the door of the cabinet after her; which door, you will bear in mind, only extended part way up, the upper portion of the aperture being covered with a "black-velvet curtain;" and, to his amazement, out thrust an "armless hand"—it was a pretty hand—"white as snow." And it, in a knowing way, "tapped him on the hand and arm." After this, faces, heads, etc., appeared; and did n't look at all ghostly either, but were perfectly natural.

Permit us to remark here, that we would suppose any such ocular demonstration, purporting to be spirit, would startle the fears of one so orthodox as we are told the narrator is; for Jesus said, to his doubting disciples, "Handle me, and see, for a spirit hath not flesh and bones as ye see me have."

Surely, the man must have forgotten his Bible, to have believed those Moravia women were spirits, after they had played the piano for him; had sung sweetest music to him; had familiarly patted him on hand and arm—ah! had embraced, "hugged, and kissed him." We say, after all this, the man must have forgotten the Scriptural declaration, "A spirit hath not flesh and bones." But do you ask for an explanation of these singular manifestations on other than spiritual development? Very well. There are times in the life of almost every one, when they are easily led into illusions. We once, out of curiosity, visited a noted French spiritualist during the *seance*. He seemed to take off his head; and then, by aid of ventriloquism, the severed parts held familiar conversation. But he as readily conversed with any friend you might wish to hear from. Now, what sane man will say those acts or tricks of the artful juggler were real? But, to hundreds of men and women, they were as real as are the late developments at Moravia, in New York. Our purpose in referring to those wonderful manifestations has been to show that necromancy has only changed in name; that its practices are common to-day, in Europe and America, under the Christian name of spiritualism; and this we have plainly done by comparative analogy. And now we are ready to examine a second proposition, namely:

2. Spiritualism is a dangerous delusion.

We wish to premise, with this thought:

Christian men seldom fall into this heresy while Christians, or, falling into it, are seldom Christians after it; and, because of this, the danger is all the more to be dreaded. It can not be denied there are men, all through the land, avowed spiritualists, who were once Christians. Fifty years ago, in this country, when men lost the grace of God out of their hearts, they were at once restless and unhappy until they returned. To-day, spiritualism seizes such men, and at once, with its semi-diabolism, settles the soul in apathetic ease, keeping up the dangerous delusion by flooding the country with pretended messages from the dead.

Isaiah said to all such: "To the law and to the testimony: if they speak not according to these words, it is because there is no life in them."

That is, as we understand the prophet, let this dispute be determined by the Word of God, which is the law.

He was now speaking of apostate Israelites (see Isaiah viii, 19), who had sought "familiar spirits, and conversed with wizards, who peeped or muttered," and declares, "If they will not go by God's word, trouble, darkness, and the dimness of anguish shall finally come upon them." The Scriptures speak elsewhere of certain characters who are given over to believe a lie that they may be damned.

Hence the danger of the delusion. It is a law in physiology, that the effect of opinion on mind is as the reality. The man who studies physical anatomy until he finds a weak spot in his frame, will at once become a chronic invalid on the physician's hands.

So men and women, falling into the power of some designing schemer, in some dark room set apart for *seance*, and seeing strange sights, their untrained ears listening to the peepings of the wizard, will first of all be put under the enchanter's spell. After that, not all the world—no, not the world's great

Redeemer—can convince them that they have not heard the voice and seen the shape of the spirits. To reason with them, and to undertake to show them the unchristlikeness of such foolish diabolism, but maddens them. Nine out of ten have a morbid, mental depression, bordering upon mania. They lose their interest in rational things. Their business goes down, and most of them go to poverty and want; for it is only the designing knaves of the circle who amass wealth by filching it from the pockets of their dupes.

At a spiritualists' picnic in Island Grove, in the East, the present season, one poor "Simple Simon" importuned the company for one hundred dollars, to enable him to perfect a wonderful invention which he claimed Hindoo and Egyptian spirits had revealed to him. They were old spirits too, some of them seven hundred years old. An old lady wanted eight hundred dollars, to help her in the performance of spiritual cures.

Nothing is more evident than that the leaders in spiritualism advocate the heresy from the most sinister motives; but it is almost equally apparent that the victims of it seldom escape the snare. Hence, we pronounce it a very dangerous delusion. But, again:

3. Spiritualism is terribly wicked and false. It is a noteworthy fact, that the advocates of heresy are flippant with Scriptural quotations, until the Scriptures condemn them; then they abandon the Bible for tradition, or for infidel productions. Spiritualists are no exception to the rule; for in argument they invariably commence with the Bible, but end with the revelations of the *seance*, and thus close the mouth of the unbeliever, for the simple reason few sensible men have been on the other side and come back to report; and respectable people, who have some regard for their reputation, do not like to go "capering" about in dark corners and dens to·hunt up

the spirits. So the argument is ended whenever the spiritualist declares himself to have had a statement from some spirit, received in some dingy back-room, where decent people would not dare to go. But we deny the right for this barest assertion, and propose showing the wickedness and falsity of the terrible heresy, by its own practices and by the Word of God, the Bible:

Deuteronomy xviii, 12: "For all that do these things are an abomination unto the Lord."

Deuteronomy xviii, 14: "For these nations, which thou shalt possess, hearkened unto observers of times, and unto diviners: but as for thee, the Lord thy God hath not suffered thee so to do."

Leviticus xix, 31: "Regard not them that have familiar spirits, neither seek after wizards, to be defiled by them."

Leviticus xx, 6: "And the soul that turneth after such as have familiar spirits, and after wizards, I have set my face against that soul, and will cut him off from among his people."

Leviticus xx, 27: "A man also or woman that hath a familiar spirit, or that is a wizard, shall surely be put to death."

Exodus xxii, 19: "Thou shalt not suffer a witch to live."

Now, read the case of Manasseh. He reigned in Israel something over fifty years; but toward the close of his reign he did that which was evil in the sight of the Lord, for which God sorely punished him.

What were his crimes? The record is in 2 Kings xxi; he became an observer of times, and used enchantment, and dealt with familiar spirits, and wrought much wickedness in the sight of the Lord. "Therefore," saith the Lord, "I am bringing such evil on Jerusalem and Judah, that whosoever heareth of it, both his ears shall tingle." The affliction came, and the poor old backslider, being in sorrow and penitence, returned unto his God. But Isaiah says: "When they shall say unto you, Seek unto them that hath familiar spirits: should not a people seek unto their God?"

Malachi, to show God's displeasure, says, "I will come near to you to judgment, and will be a swift witness against the sorcerers," etc.

"By their fruits ye shall know them," said Jesus; and by this unfailing rule may we try spiritualists.

And, first, who are spiritualists? Who, O who, in any country or town?

Second, what have they done? Has science been promoted by them? have the industries been advanced? has society been elevated and made better by spiritualists? Rather, has not the tendency been directly the reverse of all this? Those we have known have not been patterns of piety; and not one in a thousand has made any claim to the Christian religion. Robert Dale Owen, a noted infidel and free-lover, is an acknowledged light in the motley company; so is Victoria Woodhull.

Third, what are their practices? But, all known, we may not answer this question in public.

Fourth, to become a spiritualist is to abandon all Scriptural hope of heaven.

God's plan of life provides that nothing unclean, impure, or unholy can ever enter heaven.

Spiritualism admits the vilest with the pure.

God says, "Except ye repent, ye shall all likewise perish."

But spiritualism makes no difference, after death, between the good and the bad; for their professed messages from those of every grade of character, while on earth, are of the same complexion.

But Malachi says, "Then shall ye return, and discern between the righteous and the wicked, between him that serveth the Lord and him that serveth him not."

David says, "The wicked shall be turned

into hell, with all the nations that forget God;" but in the creed of the spiritualists there is no such place of habitation.

The Lord Jesus says, "These shall go away into everlasting punishment;" but the only everlasting punishment in spiritualism is possible delayed spiritual development.

God's Word says, "The soul that sinneth, it shall die;" but spiritualists deny all such Scripture, and so are without Scriptural hope of heaven.

But, to conclude, we may ask, since spiritualism can not be maintained by the Bible, but is strongly condemned wherever it is spoken of in the Scriptures, as we have plainly shown, how can a good man or woman embrace it?

It never reforms heart or life, and why should good men wish to embrace it? It helps no one in the life that now is; why, then, should men practice such folly? And, finally, it never yet smoothed a dying pillow;

why should men throw away religion for such unsatisfying chaff? May God save us from its power here, and save us in endless life hereafter, through Jesus' merit! Amen.

II.

SPIRITUALISM AN AGENCY OF SATAN.

"Get thee behind me, Satan."—JESUS.
"Neither give place to the devil."—PAUL.

THE cunning and malignity of Satan can never be fully understood in this life. But is there such a being? The name, Devil, comes to our language from the Greek word *diabolos*, which signifies calumniator, or accuser. He is represented in the Scriptures as a fallen spirit, or as a wicked angel—an enemy of the human race and a hater of God. He is in the Scriptures spoken of by the various names which express his character, such as serpent; for in that character and form he deceived the federal head. But he can assume a variety of forms, and can appear either as an angel of light or as an angel of darkness. Because of this, David calls him a dog and a fowler; Jesus calls him a wolf; he is also called a lion and an adder,—all of these names being expressive of his character.

He was not always a devil, but was created an angel of light, and of high order. How he became a devil we need not be curious to know, since the Scriptures, it must be confessed, are not very explicit on the subject. Nor have chronologists been definite as to the time.

Some time, in the unchronicled past, he became envious of Jehovah, because of God's great glory; and, being but a finite creature in knowledge, he could not know the power of God. Hence, he conceived the thought of revolt. Counseling with the unwary, he drew a multitude of heaven's inhabitants into his treasonable plot.

God suffered long and was kind; and not until Satan's treason became open revolt did he prepare the place of punishment, and cast the rebels into it.

Because of this defeat, and the consequent ruin, he became the sworn enemy of God and of man. There is nothing in the Scriptures to warrant the conclusion that Satan has aught against our race; but, being the foe of God, and seeing that God created man for his own glory, and that he has set his heart upon him to magnify him or to exalt him, he hates the man because God loves him.

But we are aware that the ever-busy mind of man is ready to ask, Did the great Author of all good, in creating all things for his own glory, also create Satan, who may very justly be styled the author of all evil; or was it by some strange transmutation in spirit-alchemy that this foe to our race came into being?

We deem the question already answered above; for the Scriptures teach plainly that he was created an angel of light. And we are ready to admit that we can only account for his wonderful transmutation on the hypothesis of angelic probation. It is a principle in the government of God, that all his intelligent creatures be perfectly happy. They could not be so unless perfectly free. They can not be free unless under law. But there can be no law without a penalty. This, we think, is evidently God's rule for the government of man, and it must have been similar in the control of angels. Satan and a host of others "kept not their first estate;" and, as man, they failed in their probation.

How long they remained in such failure, prior to the creation of man, we have no means of knowing.

But men now ask, Why did not the great and all-wise God destroy Satan? In the answer, you have the solution of the indestructibility of spirit; for the soul of God's intelligent beings can not become extinct. Hence Satan lives, and must continue to live; and while he lives will do all the evil he can.

And he will drag down to his own miserable death-home as many souls as he is able to delude. And this he will do out of revengeful hate for the God he failed to dethrone, simply because he sees the manifest love God has for man; and, he infers, to ruin man is to be avenged upon God. We are aware that all this is at variance with the vagaries of men who deny the personality of the devil; and that it is directly at variance with the Universalist's theory of the eternal pre-existence of evil, on the hypothesis of opposites, claiming a counterpart for all things; such as light—darkness; cold—heat; sweet—bitter; good—bad, etc.; thus of course defining what we call the devil as but a principle, whose opposite is God. But that such deduction is fallacious and self-contradictory, is apparent; for it refutes the plain Word of God when it says, "God is." To evade this, however, the cunning polemic assumes that, as God is, so Satan is; and this is claimed upon the above hypothesis of counterparts. If this were true, then would the fall of man by the personal temptations of an individual devil be a meaningless tissue of mythical stories, as it stands in the Bible. For, throughout all the Word of God, Satan is spoken of as an individual being separate and apart from all other beings. Plainly it is said, the angel of God disputed with the devil about the body of Moses. But when Paul spoke of fightings without, he only spoke of fears within, and said, " When I would do good, evil is present with me ;" showing this, plainly, to have a tempting devil without and an evil nature within were very different things.

Again : that the theory of the Universalist is a fallacy, is evident from the positive necessity of final disposition of the opposing forces. For the good, this is easy, assuming for it greater force and strength ; for the result of continued struggle must be the final overthrow of all evil, and must end in the triumph of all good, thus securing the completed welfare of all men. What becomes of the priority of reasoning, on the basis of opposites, Universalists have not yet told the world. Hence, the world persists in the argument, If good and evil are coeval, then they must be coexistent; and since John saw "the great dragon cast out, who is called Satan, that old serpent, the devil, who deceiveth the whole world" (see Rev. xii, 9), the Christian world continues to believe the Scriptural declaration, "Resist the devil, and he will flee from you," and are careful to heed Paul's counsel, "Neither give place to the devil."

But again, as already intimated, we infer the distinctive individuality and personality of the devil, from the names given him in God's Word, all of which are expressive of his personality. In Revelation ix, 11, he is called the "angel of the bottomless pit." In John xii, 31, he is said to be the "prince of this world;" but in Ephesians he is called the "prince of darkness." Many Scriptures set forth the low, vicious, cunning boldness with which he tries to drag down the souls of men; for, while the Bible uses the definite article *the* to describe Satan, it must be understood that he is not alone in his work of diabolism, for there are whole troops of devils.

> "They throng the air, they darken heaven,
> And rule this lower world."

Matthew and Luke give an account, in their Gospels, of one possessed with devils; and the plural is most used in the New Testament Scriptures when they speak of those possessed of the devil. Out of Mary Magdalene Jesus cast seven; and in the country of the Gergesenes those cast out were called legion, because they were many.

But all these, it must be noted, were subordinate to Satan, who was their ruinous counselor in heaven, and whose fortunes they have been doomed to follow. And by these assistants he carries on, in every age, an unrelenting warfare upon our race. The trail of the serpent is left on every page of the history of the past, and the evidence of his operations is seen through the whole course of earthly affairs. In the Christian age, "the mystery of iniquity" is the center of his system. Opposition to the cross of Christ is its leading characteristic; but its modifications are innumerable.

We give Catholicism full credit for all the iniquity of which her mysteries are author; but we can not regard Popery as fully answering the description of "the mystery of iniquity" in its maturity, as set forth in the Scriptures. Popery may be the highest type of it, and we think it is; but Paul said, in his day, "The mystery of iniquity doth already work." Catholicism, as we see it, was not known to Paul; but "the mystery of iniquity" was then working ruin. And from that day to this, each generation has witnessed some new feature of the predicted abomination. Delusions and corruptions have crept in, and multiplied around us. Hostility to the Gospel is found in systems, opinions, and practices subversive of the true faith, sufficient to startle the advocate of salvation through faith in Jesus Christ. It is true, these evil devices of Satan are as yet disjointed and various; but the fear is, they will eventually coalesce and constitute an infamous whole, under the leadership of Satan. In the memory of the present generation, many sects of antagonistic principles have become united. Usually, this occurs by the strong swallowing up the weak. And to-day Popery, in true gamboge style, is making giant efforts to absorb all there is of strength and beauty in the Protestant Episcopal Church. With this, Satan would be in triumph; but in other departments, and with other Christian Churches, he can not hope to succeed in this direction. Hence, his resort to other means with which to work "the mystery of iniquity." And what, among Christians, could do the work better than contention and strife? For the destruction and overthrow of nationalities, he uses these most; but for the ruin of Christian Churches he uses heresy, false and dangerous doctrines, even doctrines of devils. Of this the apostle gives due warning when he says, "The Spirit speaketh expressly that in the latter times some shall depart from the faith, giving heed to seducing spirits and doctrines of devils;" or, as the last word should be rendered, "demons." It would then read, Giving heed to seducing spirits and doctrines of demons, or the emissaries of Satan. The word *diabolos*, from which the name devil is derived, is never used in the plural when applied to Satan. So, whenever the word "devils" occurs in the New Testament, it should be understood as demons, or as inferior fallen angels, subject to Satan. And now, in this aspect of the workings of "the mystery of iniquity," what more aptly illustrates it than spiritualism, as known in modern days?

A liberality of sentiment has been allowed to find place among nominal Christians, that sees, in the idolatry of the nations, accepted worship of the true God, under different symbols; and thus they not only legalize all forms of worship, but approve idol worship. This is in direct opposition to the plain Word of God; for it every-where condemns false gods with holy severity, speaking of them, in terms of indignation and contempt, under such titles as "abominations," "no gods," "shame," "stocks," "stones," "vanities," "devils." The heathen worshiped a multitude of such. What correct thought could they have of Deity? For, in common reason we may argue, every deity they had, above one, was an evidence of their ignorance of the true God of heaven and earth, and showed beyond cavil that they had no true knowledge of the "one true God over all." To this must be added the gross and sensual conceptions in their minds of their images and deities, the amours, lusts, quarrels, and many other mean qualities, which they attributed to their gods. We shall by this, we think, see plainly that the heathen world has no true knowledge of God, as he is to the Christian revealed in revelation and nature.

But it may be necessary, to clear our way for the discussion of the true character of spiritualism, to consider the words *devil* and *demon* more fully. Let us, then, give attention to the use of the terms, both in Scripture and in that class of ancient writings known as the classics.

In Homer, the demons and gods of the heathen always mean the same, and the words are used interchangeably. And while we admit that the application of the word was sometimes modified, yet it is worthy of note the identity was never lost sight of.

The Greek philosophers speak of demons as an intermediate class between gods and men, calling them either gods or demons according as they understood them to send blessing or cursing on their subjects. Their superior gods were not supposed to send either cursing or blessing upon men, nor in any way to interfere with the affairs of earth. Because of this view of the gods, the masses were given almost wholly to demon-worship. Fear being the moving impulse, the evil demons must be propitiated. But they also deified warriors, philosophers, and heroes; and this, doubtless, was what first led in that age to the application of the word *demon* to the souls of the dead.

Plato did not relinquish the original meaning of the word, but he attached a new meaning to it; for he calls the souls of disembodied men demons, and seems to have some vague reference to the original creation of man in the image of God. This Platonic use of the term gradually prevailed, at times nearly excluding its original or earlier sense. Josephus, in his "Jewish Wars," following this interpretation, says, "Those that we call demons are the spirits of wicked men."

Thus we find, in classical usage, first, demons were regarded as gods, holding intermediate place between men and other or higher gods; and, second, they were the souls of deceased men. The good and evil demon, spoken of by Socrates, seems to have reference only to the conscience bearing witness for or against us.

When the word occurs in the Old or New Testament, we might reasonably look to find it very much modified.

Thus, in Deuteronomy xxxii, 17, it is said: "They sacrificed unto devils [demons], not to God; to gods whom they knew not, to new gods that came newly up, whom your fathers feared not."

Paul doubtless refers to this sin, when

reproving the Corinthians for mingling heathen rites with Christian ordinances, saying, "The Gentiles sacrifice to demons and to God, and I would not that ye should have fellowship with demons."

The word was used by the Athenians, as signifying inferior deities, when they said of Paul, "He seemeth to be a setter forth of strange gods;" and as Paul stood on Mars' Hill for the defense of the truth, he said, "I perceive that in all things ye are too superstitious." Good authority claims that this might have been rendered, "In all things ye are much given to demon-worship." And this would have given no offense; for the Greeks would have understood it as an implied, but mild, reproof of over-zeal, demon-worshiper being understood in Athens as a pious man. As we have shown, they employed the term as interchangeable, expressing either the fear of God or the fear of demons.

But the word demons, in the New Testament Scriptures, often expresses definitely malignant spirits. Such terms as the following establish this: "unclean spirits," "spirits of wickedness," "evil spirits."

The gods worshiped by the heathen, in Paul's day, were certainly believed to be really-existing evil demons; for they applied this very name to the beings they worshiped; and the accusation of the Jews, that Jesus cast out devils by Beelzebub, the prince of devils—or demons, by the prince of demons—appears conclusive as to the sense in which the word was employed. The reply of the Lord sanctions this understanding. In like manner, when the Seventy returned, and reported that even the devils were subject to them through his name, Jesus replied, saying, "I beheld Satan falling from heaven as lightning."

Well, it is affirmed with very great confidence by spiritualists, that they are, in this the nineteenth century, in easy and direct communication with spirits; that they converse with them, and receive most interesting information from them of the state of the dead in particular, and of the spirit-world in general.

That they are in communication with spirits, we allow. But two things we deny to spiritualists throughout these pages: First, that they hold any kind of intercourse in their *seances* with the spirits of the dead, or the souls of those who once lived on the earth in mortal bodies; and, second, that they ever receive any trustworthy or reliable information, from the spirits answering their call, of the spirit-world, because, as we have indicated and shall plainly prove, the spirits answering such call are lying spirits, or demons. We have admitted they are in spirit-communication with spirits, and are ready also to admit that they do, by the various spiritual mediums or channels of spirit-communication, receive messages from those spirits;

but those spirits, we are sure, are—as we have said—demons, and are full of lies.

For many years, like hosts of honest Christians, being alarmed at this species of diabolism, we tried to keep it out of sight, to explain it away, to shame it down, by calling it jugglery, tricks, sleight of hand, etc.; but, after thorough study, we have become convinced that all attempts to explain the phenomena of spiritualism by the operation of natural laws are wholly futile and unsatisfactory. And though it be true there is much of low cunning, knavery, jugglery, and sleight of hand practiced with it, for the purpose of gain and for other reasons, yet the name and character, the intelligence and learning, of some of its adherents, forbid us to call in question the statements they make. Nor can we in many cases pronounce it jugglery.

The contradictions of some of the spirits do not prove there were no spirits present; they may only prove the bungling work of the medium, or performer. If the spirit of Wesley or of Calvin is made to utter a blasphemy in one circle in New York, and to pronounce a blessing in a circle in Chicago, while it tells political lies at the same time in St. Louis, it proves most certainly that the spirits of Wesley and Calvin were not present in any of those circles; but it by no means proves that the blasphemy, blessing, and political falsehoods did not have a spirit author in each circle.

The Word of God plainly gives warning that men will give heed to seducing spirits, and to the teachings of evil demons. And if the manifestations of spiritualism should become tenfold more startling than any thing it has yet shown to the world, it would only be in accordance with what the Scriptures affirm is to precede the time of the end; for the coming of the wicked one is, as Paul sets it forth, "after the working of Satan, with all power and signs and lying wonders"—the last expression referring not to spurious miracles, but to miracles performed in support of falsehood. Again, it is said of Satan, "He doeth great wonders, so that he maketh fire come down from heaven in the sight of men, and deceiveth them that dwell on the earth by those miracles which he had power to do." Need we marvel if the approach of that consummation of ungodliness be marked with "the mystery of iniquity" and startling impostures? And who, in the face of these Scriptural warnings, will fail to see in modern spiritualism, with its recent manifestations, that "the mystery of iniquity doth already work?"

Let us remember we have been faithfully warned of these impostures; and let us be guarded against them. For there shall arise false Christs in those days, say the Scriptures, and false prophets, who shall show signs and wonders, insomuch that if it were possible they would deceive the very elect. Behold, says the Divine witness, "I have told you." We must not be supposed to believe that any thing so stupid and bungling as spiritualism is, can be the complete fulfillment of these solemn warnings; but it is evidently a warning to the watchful believer as to the source of danger to the cause of Christ.

Nor are we, as Christians, to treat this monstrous iniquity with simple contempt; for it has power—power that is acknowledged in God's Word; power that is all the more dangerous because of its hidden mysteries; power to deceive and then destroy. Few, if any, even of earth's wisest thinkers, can withstand this power of demons, unless they be aided by an abiding and saving faith in Jesus Christ. Is it not true that men of master minds, with all the mental culture that earth could give, have fallen before this Juggernaut of devils, as readily as the tender reed goeth down before the tempest? Witness the scholarly Robert Dale Owen, and many others of greater strength of mind and of purer morals, to say nothing of the hundreds and thousands of ordinary minds, who, like the tiny minnows of the deep, have gone with the great leviathans down to moral death. Ah! if we could stop here, then the danger would be less alarming. But, alas! multitudes of Christians, and even Christian ministers, have been numbered with its ruined victims; and to-day the earth witnesses the sad spectacle of men who once claimed to feel the vows of God upon them, and who were not disobedient to the heavenly calling, but, feeling a Christ-like burden for souls, were wont to go forth in the name of the Master, striving to make the world better by pointing it to the Lamb of God, but now advocating the doctrines of the prince of darkness, on no other authority than that they are wholly unable to explain the demon-like apparitions of the dark *seance* of modern spiritualism. One such fallen minister, of Unitarian faith, was wont to teach in the name of Jesus in this city; but, alas! the dark, damning snare of demonology tangled his feet and strangled his love for the ministry of the Gospel of Christ, supplanting it with strong admiration for "the mystery of iniquity;" and now, instead of preaching Christ to the people, he strongly advocates spiritualism. And others of this city, and all through the land, good lay members of the Church of Christ, have become sadly entangled in this hateful net of Satan, so much so that their faith in Jesus Christ as a Savior has become shaken.

It is sad to consider the change this moral bane has wrought in such victims. Once they were active members of the Church of God, delighting to do him service; but, from the day that the poison of spiritualism entered their souls, they have been as barren of spiritual duty as of spiritual enjoyment.

And now, in conclusion of this chapter, suffer a word of exhortation. Can we, as

Christians, and especially as Christian ministers, stand, with hands folded, idly by, and see this great mystery of evil ruin our people, as it creeps stealthily in, doing its hellish work in the dark? Nay, let us take the alarm. "The mystery of iniquity is already beginning to work." Let us, in the name of morality and religion, make ourselves masters of the mystery, by study, faith, and prayer; and let us give timely warning. Thus many may be saved from its damning power, for our encouragement in the work. Let us remember that, as in apostolic days, Satan can not stand before the name of Jesus, whenever that name is used in faith and sincerity. "Jesus I know," said the devil, on one occasion; and in the name of Jesus may we conquer spiritualism, which is but a manifestation of Satan's power.

> "Jesus, the name high over all,
> In hell or earth or sky;
> Angels and men before it fall,
> And devils fear and fly.

Jesus, the name to sinners dear,
   The name to sinners given,—
It scatters all their guilty fears,
   It turns their hell to heaven.

Jesus the prisoner's fetters breaks,
   And bruises Satan's head;
Power into strengthless souls he speaks,
   And life into the dead."

III.

SPIRITUALISM AND DEMONOLOGY.

"But I fear, lest by any means, as the serpent beguiled Eve through his subtlety, so your minds should be corrupted from the simplicity that is in Christ."—2 Cor. xi, 3.

WE have, in the former pages of these lectures, identified spiritualism with the work of Satan. We now come to speak of it directly as an agency of demons. We are aware that many good and wise men, with a holy horror for strife and a timid fear of agitation, are wont to regard this dangerous heresy as an innocent or harmless something that time will cure, hence there is no need of meeting it with argument. But, Christian reader, just look about you for one moment at the ruin it has wrought, before you hastily pass judgment upon it as an innocent delusion.

How many, who were once Christians, and were happy, are now the dupes and advocates of this delusion! How many families in this Christian land have had the domestic peace of the family band hopelessly destroyed by this doctrine of devils! for it will not be denied that it panders to all that is carnal in our race.

Universalism teaches the final salvation and happiness of all mankind; but it earnestly enjoins chastity, virtue, and the sanctity of the conjugal relation, in the life that now is. And because of these virtues, they are really valuable accessions to any community; for their leaders not only teach good morals, but practice it in their every-day life, and some of them are model patterns of uprightness. And yet orthodox Christians feel perfect license to cry out against their heresy, and to warn them of the dangers of a hell which multitudes of honest Christian Universalists will never find.

But here is a doctrine of devils, believed in and practiced by men and women of every grade of morals and intellect, a doctrine which strikes at the very foundation of human society, and destroys the bonds of human happiness, because it destroys the family tie, or disregards the marriage relation. That it has done and is doing all this, none conversant with its workings will deny. Events, under the spiritualistic teaching of Robert Dale Owen and the accomplished Fanny Wright, at New Harmony, Ind., can not be forgotten, by many citizens of Ohio, Indiana, and Illinois, to this day. They are certainly remembered in New Harmony. Events of similar character have occurred elsewhere—yea, are transpiring now—under the same baneful doctrine of demons, and its sister heresy, free-loveism; for they were brooded by the same demon. Especially is it true, now, in the State of New York, in Louisville, Ky., as well as many other places in the United States, in London, and nearly all over Europe.

Is it a time, we ask, for silence? Nay, as we are to watch for souls, let us raise the alarm by crying out to the people, "Neither give place to the devil." For we may be assured that something more potent than silent contempt is necessary, if we would see spiritualism overthrown. It must be met, firmly and logically, with Scriptural and reasonable argument, if we would save reasonable men and women from its delusive power. The phenomena are as startling and bewildering to the intellect of the refined and educated as its doctrines are pleasing to the affections and passions of the depraved men and women who gloat over its disclosures.

But its advocates err when they assert it as new or novel. Its practices were as largely indulged in, in the days of Moses, as they are to-day; and the sin of necromancy was as sternly denounced in the Word of God then as was the sin of adultery in the days of Jesus.

If, then, the Bible treats it so gravely, let us calmly but firmly consider the subject.

The fall of man was no mere accident; but was the result of a well-developed plot for his ruin, conceived with intelligence, and executed with great skill. The being who devised it has since gradually brought man under a malignant system of delusion, and has ever evinced a deep and infernal design against God and man. And O, how cunningly are his plans designed for the ensnaring of the human soul! Whether we look at the pagan, Jewish, or Christian systems, we every-where see corrupt panderings to the solicitations of depravity, all ministering to the pride, folly, and selfishness of fallen man. This, of itself, ought to convince every rational mind that the designer and executor of such skillful snare must be directly opposite to the source of all good; and this opposite, we maintain, is Satan. And we rejoice that we have an infallible guide in establishing both the existence and character of demons; for there is a being whose dark deeds and malicious operations are frequently referred to by inspired writers, called by them the devil; and to question his existence is simply to confess ourselves his dupes.

We have given, in a former chapter, something of the Bible account of the original life and position of Satan and his angels, or comrades and assistants; but we may farther quote from Jude. He says, of demons, "The angels which kept not their first estate, but left their own habitation, he hath reserved in everlasting chains under darkness unto the judgment of the great day." And Peter says, "God spared not the angels that sinned, but cast them down to hell, and delivered them into chains of darkness." Of Satan, Christ said he was a murderer from the beginning, and abode not in the truth.

From these and kindred Scriptures we deduce the following facts:

1. The devil and his angels were once holy intelligences in heaven, but fell from their original condition. They once stood in holy purity before God, and fulfilled the end of their creation. But they were soon involved in wretchedness and ruin; for they abode not in the truth. They sinned. "They kept not their first estate." They left their former habitation; but did not, could not, go beyond Jehovah's power. By creation, then, they were highly exalted; and, because of this exaltation, their terrible fall is all the more appalling.

2. But, it is also evident, they were, in their creation and first position, free agents; and this is the ground of their condemnation. "They kept not their first estate." This, of necessity, implies perfect moral freedom. Satan became the father of lies, from choice. He and his angels are voluntary transgressors.

The actions of a being destitute of volition must forever be free alike from praise and blame. Satan and his comrades sinned, and thus became the voluntary instruments of their own fall.

3. They are reserved in darkness, to be punished at the Judgment of the Great Day. Their present abode is hell. The Greek term is *Tartarus*. Robinson's Greek Lexicon defines Tartarus as the abyss of *Hades*, where the shades of the wicked are imprisoned and tormented. M'Knight speaks of it as a deep place under the earth; but the Greeks spoke of Tartarus as in the air, or as airy Tartarus. This term, then, as used by the apostle Peter, would not only give the idea of a place of punishment for wicked spirits, but would by many be understood as being in the air. And this agrees with the general idea of the Bible; for the Old Testament represents Satan as going up and down in the earth, tempting men. The New Testament gives the same

idea. He walketh about as a roaring lion; and he is called the prince of the power of the air. We are said to wrestle, not with flesh and blood, but with the rulers of the darkness of this world, and with spiritual wickedness in high places. This must be understood as direct contests with demons who inhabit the air. But whether this be their usual abode, authors are not agreed, nor is it an essential difference; for, whatever be the present abode of fallen spirits or demons, it is evident they have not yet met their final doom, for they are reserved in chains to the Day of Judgment to be punished. This is proven by their memorable inquiry of Jesus, "Art thou come hither to torment us before the time?" Chains of darkness, then, must be understood simply to restrain them in their degraded state. And this shows their fallen estate in terrible contrast to their former place. Once they were angels of light, free to range the domain of light, but now "reserved in chains of darkness." And though Satan can for a purpose appear as an angel of light, yet even then his true abode is darkness. Once more: chains of darkness do not confine the devil and his angels to any certain spot or place, but simply to a certain condition.

We get the character of Satan from the names given him in the Scriptures. He is called an adversary, an enemy, a tempter, a deceiver, a murderer, and a liar. Surely, from these characteristic titles we may know his character; for if it were possible to combine all that is foul and false in one being, it would not be more hideous than the character given to Satan in the Holy Scriptures. And, most certainly, every true Christian heart on earth must recoil from the slightest touch of this subtle, false accuser of God and man. The very mention of his name in connection with the acts of men should at once raise the alarm. But is it not a sad reflection, that he is not only consulted as a "familiar spirit," and his aid invoked in the furtherance of devilish lusts, but his communications to the *seance*, given in person to the medium, or else revealed by some one of his legion helpers, is preferred to all Scripture and all intelligence and reason?

Most certainly, no Christian could be induced to take part in the dark circle with spiritualists, if they were apprised of the fiendish character of the "familiar spirits" consulted. But it is the province of Satan to hold his subjects in the dark. And, since it is true that Satan and his devilish helpers were in being before our world began, they have been acquainted with all who lived on the earth before us, as well as with all who live here now; it is not a marvel that they find a medium of communicatian with those who are willing to consult them. Nor is it strange that such old reporters can and do make startling revelations about the unseen world.

But it must always be borne in mind that Satan is the father of lies; yea, "is a liar from the beginning, and the truth is not in him." If he were an unskillful bungler, then he need not be dreaded; but, alas! he is full of cunning art, and is an able debater. The Scriptures represent him as securing his infamous objects by guile and deception. And this ingenuity is what is to be dreaded; for he has no power to compel obedience to his will, not even over the weakest child of grace.

It ought to be an alarming fact to spiritualists, that no medium ever thinks of asking God's blessing on the "circle," in the name of the Lord Jesus. We are willing to assert that, if any medium—so called—will, before sitting down at the *seance*, earnestly invoke the presence of God, in faith and sincerity, and then receive any kind of communication from "familiar spirits," we shall be ready to recant much that we have written in these pages. We are willing to stand pledged to this; for, in all cases where God is acknowledged, Satan has no power. Had he resorted to coercive force in the instance of the Fall, the effort must have been a failure; but, by subtlety and deception, his success was readily accomplished. True, he announced a falsehood that was alarming; but that falsehood was made plausible by ingenious reasoning. It ought to be kept in mind by all generations, that when Satan holds any communication with mortals, it is in a false character. He came to Eve in the body of a serpent, and assumed great wisdom. His announcement was, Eat of this forbidden tree, and ye shall be as God. This seemed desirable, and the snare was a success.

To the infidel, he comes in the dark, dismal body of the charnel-house, asserting "death an eternal sleep." But man's every impulse cries out against annihilation. Satan, in argument, holds up the rottenness and corruption of the grave, and demands, " Can these bones live?" and the skeptic is confirmed.

To the scientist, he comes in the form of science and reason, and plausibly argues "the eternal pre-existence of matter;" and this, by the materialist, is accepted as more reasonable than revelation.

But in every age he comes to the restless, longing souls of those who are unwilling to serve God, but who are not willing to stifle the hungry longing within them for the spirit-life, in the form of "familiar spirits;" and, by pretended messages from the dead and revelations of the unseen spirit-world, he is enabled to gain full possession of the mind and reason of the poor unfortunate spirit, to the ruin of the soul; for, after that, his only oracle is spiritualism. And this is Satan's wisdom, to blind the eyes of men's understanding. O, how false and subtle is he! Falsehood and deceit are his chosen instruments for securing the present and eternal ruin of our race.

In all heathen lands, he rules the masses with cruelest despotic power. Even in measurably enlightened pagan nations, their oracles are but caricatures of consulting the God of heaven, largely mixed, it is true, with human trickery. But in this way the ruler of darkness secures, in all heathen nations, the undivided homage of both the deceiver and the deceived.

The systems of divination used by such nations are fearful engines of mischief; for they enslave and degrade every faculty of the soul. Nor is there material difference in the incantations used by them from the means employed by spiritualists in Christian lands. Pagans, in their divinations, predict future events by the air, by the planets, by the flight of birds, by the inspection of the human hand, and by various other equally foolish means. But these are without a knowledge of God's Word. Hence, Satan holds them captive by his will, without resort to the revelation of the Scriptures of Divine truth. For it is characteristic of Satan's strategy to adapt his work to the means in the hands of the people, or to gauge his operations by the intelligence of the people he would destroy. It is comparatively easy for him to control the dark and beclouded mind of the heathen and pagan; but in all Christian lands there is a knowledge of the Holy Scriptures, revealing to men a knowledge of the spirit-world and the true state of the souls of the departed. Hence, to make his fiendish work a success in such lands, he must pervert the Word of God; and this he does, with both cunning and wisdom. Witness his flippant and unwarranted quotation and interpretation of Scripture, made to Jesus, when he was exhausting all his skill in tempting him. And are not all spiritualists as profuse in their quotations and interpretations of the Word of God? Yea, many leading spiritualists are avowed exponents of the Scriptures.

But it will doubtless be asked by the advocates of the *seance*, Is there any proof that spirits have any thing to do with the systems of divination practiced by the heathen? We answer, the proof is plainly given in the sixteenth chapter of the Acts of the Apostles. The spirit in the maiden was a spirit of divination, and carried on the work of deception by instructing the damsel in the art of his science, or in soothsaying. The spirit that possessed her also knew the character of the apostles, and indorsed them as servants of the most high God; and it even acknowledged them as teachers of the way of salvation—the purpose being, no doubt, to pervert such teaching, by mixing with it the doctrines of devils. This grieved Paul sorely; and he, in the name of Christ, rejected such testimony, and commanded the spirit to come out of the young woman, which it did, to the dismay of her masters; "for by her soothsaying she brought much gain to her masters."

The power of Satan to corrupt Christianity is recognized in all the Epistles to the early Churches. The first manifestations of this was by false or Judaizing teachers, substituting the deeds of the law for the righteousness of Christ. Paul seems to be the first to detect the infernal source of such teaching, and gives the alarm in the eleventh chapter of 2 Corinthians, saying: "But I fear, lest by any means, as the serpent beguiled Eve through his subtlety, so your minds should be corrupted from the simplicity that is in Christ. . . . For such are false apostles, deceitful workers, transforming themselves into the apostles of Christ. And no marvel; for Satan himself is transformed into an angel of light. Therefore it is no great thing if his ministers also be transformed as the ministers of righteousness; whose end shall be according to their works."

Here, then, is plain evidence of the power of Satan, through the medium of men, to corrupt even the Gospel of Christ. Let spiritualists who bring new doctrines from the spirits of the dead, as they suppose, beware. Such falsities are from no departed spirit of any mortal who ever lived on this earth, but are from fallen spirits, or demons, who only seek to pervert the way of salvation into a lie, by substituting a gospel of their own. Should not the words of warning given by St. Paul be tremblingly heeded by all who are tempted to tamper with the spirits of demons? Hear Paul, in Galatians i, 8: "Though we, or an angel from heaven, preach any other gospel unto you than that we have preached unto you, let him be accursed."

But, notwithstanding the apostle's warning, Satan succeeded in corrupting the Gospel, by setting in motion "the mystery of iniquity," which led to most blasphemous apostasy. This apostasy was manifested in the early ages of Christianity, in the form of works, penance, etc., much of which has entered into and remains in the Catholic Church. Praying to the holy virgin, to saints, and bowing to images, have no other origin. But Satan, seeing that this was not sufficient corruption of the Gospel of Christ, and that many Catholics were true Christians, despite those great errors—and seeing, too, that millions would never be corrupted through the Satanic heresies of Catholicism—"the mystery of iniquity" must work outside of that great Church organization, as well as within it. Hence, the characteristics of this dark mystery are seen to thicken in the Protestant world, in every age.

It is now the boast of the dupes of this heresy of demons, that their numbers are increasing annually—not realizing that the increase of this mysterious abomination is another proof of the truth of the Bible, which points specifically to the multiplication of signs and lying wonders, especially in the last days.

If Satan put it into the hearts of Ananias

and his wife to lie even unto God, we may infer there is nothing too dark or damning for him to do. The proof of the inspired declaration, that the god of this world has blinded the eyes of the people, is on every hand; and among the very strongest proofs of this is the increase of spiritualism. Nothing but the pure Gospel of Christ is able to meet it.

IV.

SPIRITUALISM AN AGENCY OF SATAN.

"Jesus I know, and Paul I know; but who are ye?"
ACTS XIX, 15.

THROUGHOUT the Dark Ages, when the simplicity of the Gospel of Jesus was corrupted by gross admixture of superstition and paganism, the popular mind was ruled by superstitious awe, and terror of ghosts, hobgoblins, necromancy, and witchcraft. It was the constant effort of Satan to pervert the light of the Gospel of Christ, and to turn science and philosophy against the very means by which the mind of the student had been enlightened for the successful pursuit of them. Hence, all belief in the supernatural and spiritual must be rejected as unphilosophical, illogical, and incorrect. Partly by the Reformation, but mainly by the unsatisfied longing, and the bitter wailings of humanity for a spirit-life beyond, has this heresy of Satan and the infidel been, in modern days, suppressed and hushed up. And all the old, corrupt superstitions of materialism have been revived; and to-day we witness the anomalous spectacle of the very characters who once called it childish and the weakness of folly to believe in the spirit-life, not only the avowed advocates of it, but, with all the desperation of despair, invoking the evidence of demons to prove something tangible regarding the disembodied soul of humanity.

The question between Christians and this sect of infidels, who go by the pleasing name of spiritualists, is not about the possibility of spirit-communication, but about the character of such communication. Christians have ever allowed the ministration of spirits, and have also understood the power of Satan in holding the souls of men captive at his will.

But the quarrel is between this class and themselves, when they wrote on the tombstones of their own children, "Death is an eternal sleep."

The Word of God plainly teaches there are legions of evil spirits, or demons, who are ever ready to answer the call of those who invoke their presence; for thus they are doing the pleasure of their chief, in perverting the grace of God and deluding the souls of men.

The claim of the spiritualists, that spirits answer their call in the darkness of the *seance*, will not be denied by any who have made themselves familiar with the many Scriptural expositions of the dark and damning deeds of demons. Jesus and his apostles frequently came in contact with those who were possessed of demons. We are aware that some pretenders have assumed to defend revelation, by explaining such demoniacal possession as only the result of natural disorder, or of physical derangement. But all such attempted explanation is at the expense of the Divine Word itself; for it explains away the express language of inspiration. And thus, in their bungling attempts to explain a mystery, they unconsciously exhibit the Lord Jesus and his apostles as confirming the superstitions of the age; for they recognized Satanic possessions wherever they met them—yea, and they were also recognized by the demons of possession. All through the New Testament Scriptures this is found true. Divination and soothsaying, telling of things unseen, and foretelling future events, are all characteristics of demoniacal spirits.

There are two forcible examples given by the evangelists, that forbid the evasions to which we have referred. Bishop Warburton aptly remarks: "Our indulgent Master has been pleased to guard this important truth against the most plausible evasions of self-conceited men, to cut off all escape from a forced concession of the mighty hand of God, compelling his most averse creatures to acknowledge his sovereign power. One of those cases is the temptation of Jesus by the devil in the wilderness; the other is the possession of brute animals." The Savior of men, with all the infirmities of our race as a man, was nevertheless the victim of no bodily disorder or physical ailment; and he was on this occasion subject to the buffetings of Satan, and only by his Divinity was able to overcome the Satanic power that assailed him. Nor can it be argued, as some have supposed, with those who were the victims of Satan's power, that he was under any kind of mental delusion; for the infinite mind of the Messiah was far above all such suspicion. But the evidence of the power and presence of demons, in the case of the Gaderenes and the swine, is equally forcible; for they at once recognized Jesus as the Christ, and besought him, if they were cast out, to be permitted to enter the swine.

We will not argue that a diseased mind may not conjure up all manner of chimeras and delusive, startling things; but, most certainly, none will assume that any such mental aberration afflicted a great herd of swine all at the same time, and instantly, so that they simultaneously rushed to their own ruin in the sea. Plainly, we are driven to admit both the presence and power of the demons, or deny the authenticity of the whole narrative; for the brutish instinct of the animals could never have moved them thus, in harmony, to hurry to their own destruction.

But, if further evidence of the presence and possession of demons be desired, it may be stated they were ever subject to the name of Christ. Take the case given in Acts xix, 14. There were seven impostors, who had doubtless discovered the truth of the statement we have just made, and seeing that devils were subject to the order of Paul when he used the name of the Lord Jesus, and finding a man possessed, they determined, either for the public notoriety it would give them, or for gain, to imitate Paul. Accordingly, in the name of Jesus, whom Paul preached, they commanded the unclean spirits to come out of the man. They—the spirits—recognized the name of Paul and of Jesus, but refused to recognize the authority of these impostors to use such names; and they were insulted and roused to fury at the audacity and imposition of the men. They terribly frightened the hypocrites; for the man possessed leaped upon them and overcame them, so that they were glad to escape without their clothes, being wounded.

If it be objected that these cases have nothing to do with modern spiritualism, we answer, they prove beyond dispute that demons can act through the human organization; that they not only can do so, but actually have made both men and women mediums of utterance and actions. The fact of their doing so now may be plainly inferred. Bear in mind, in all cases demonology has been practiced in opposition to the Word of God, beginning with Satan's contradictions in the Garden of Eden, and coming down to the sorcery of Simon Magus and Elymas. In all cases, each act of the demon has been in flagrant opposition to the Word of God. And another noted feature of demonism is this: wherever God's presence is invoked, demons have no power. We have asserted, in a former chapter, that no spiritual "circle" dare invoke the blessed presence of the living God in their nightly sessions. Such invocation would be disastrous to the revelations of the spirits. And wherefore? we ask. Ah! those dark spirits know the power of the living God; and, because of that power, they are not likely to put in an appearance where such presence is first sought. And now, if we are correct—and spiritualists will not deny it—may we not infer—yea, may we not assume positively—the spirits who answer the call of the medium are not the spirits of those who, like ourselves, once lived on the earth encumbered with mortal bodies? for they, by the teachings of spiritualism, are now in paradise, and ought to have no occasion to fear the presence of God. For it must be remembered that spiritualists claim to receive communications from the spirits of those who all their lives professed to love God, and who, dying in the true faith of the Gospel of Christ, went in holy triumph to possess the spirit-land. Surely, these will not be afraid to visit the circle where God's blessing and his presence is sought in prayer. Why, then, O deluded spiritualist! why not pray to the God of revelation, when you sit down in the dark *seance* for mere fragmentary revelations of the spirit-world? Ah! the argument is against you. The spirits that answer your call are demons, who only reveal things to you as their father, the devil, instructs or permits. And, as he is the father of lies, you dare not with safety put any confidence in the communications he may permit you to receive.

We have already taught in these pages that the Scriptures nowhere authorize the belief that the spirits of departed men, and especially of good men, ever held communication with mortals on earth, through the medium of spiritualism. There is, however, one exception, and it is the case of Samuel and Saul. It is plainly stated that Samuel appeared unto Saul at the instance of the witch of En-dor. We stated this case in our chapter on Spiritualism and Necromancy; but as we have now assumed the ground that only the spirits of demons answer the call of the spiritual medium in the *seance*, we deem it proper to consider more fully this only exception. And we note, first, the medium, or witch, did not herself expect the veritable person of Samuel to appear. She doubtless supposed that, as usual, some demoniacal spirit would answer her call, who would personify the dead prophet, Samuel, and who would, by his deceptive cunning, delude Saul, and bring gain to her; but when she realized that it was Samuel who appeared, she was the worst scared witch that ever held *seance* in spiritual circle on this earth. Whether she had been acquainted with the prophet in his life-time, and thus was enabled to recognize him on sight, or whether the spirit of some demon revealed to her both Samuel and Saul, we can not tell; but we do know that, as soon as Samuel appeared, she was enabled to see through the disguise of Saul. That there is not profound mystery in the whole transaction, will not be assumed; or that we can unravel the mystery by any logic of Scripture or reason, we will not claim. It may have been that some demon was enabled or permitted to take possession of the well-known frame of the dead prophet—or, what seems more likely to us, was permitted to assume some spectral semblance of the man of God, and also to mimic the familiar sound of the prophet's voice, and thus deceive the wretched king and the terribly frightened woman. But, whether the one or the other of these be true, we can not suppose that the repose of this servant of God could be broken, either by the wickedness of Saul or the incantations of the witch.

There is nothing in it all to prove the false claim of spiritualism, that the spirits of the dead speak to the living through the spiritual medium; for the form of the prophet is seen, and his voice is heard, as though he were personally present. And there is not the slightest indication that the spirit of the prophet was speaking through the person of the medium, or of the presence of invisible agency.

Witchcraft often took the form of necromancy, or pretended consultation of the dead. The heathen, to this day, pretend to call up the dead by their incantations. But God's Word gives no countenance to the supposition that the spirits of the dead answer such call. It does, however, abundantly prove the agency of evil spirits, not only among Jews and idolators, but also among professed Christians.

As soon as "the mystery of iniquity" began to work, we find the agency of demons at work, as busily as among the heathen in the days of the prophets, striving often to counterfeit the gifts of the Holy Ghost. Paul, meeting this dangerous heresy of demons, gave the alarm, by exhorting the brethren to believe not every spirit, but to try the spirits, and see whether they be of God. Because of the persistence of demons in their efforts to counteract the effect of the Gospel of Christ, it became necessary to give warning of the great sin of consulting "familiar spirits" and seeking intercourse with the dead. Paul enumerates, as a work of the flesh, witchcraft, and adds, "They that do such things shall not inherit the kingdom of God."

It is not surprising that a benighted heathen should have faith in witchcraft and divination; but is it not a matter of astonishment that an intelligent being, in a Christian land, in this age of culture and science, should bow down to the same stupid work of devils? The vague, unsatisfying reports of those modern diviners about the spirit-world, not to speak of their frequent contradictory character, we would suppose would be enough to convince an intelligent mind of the absurdity of spiritualism, as known in our day. But that men, with an open Bible in their hands, revealing, in flashing light, the indignation of Jehovah against all who do such things, will yet persist in such practices, is to us unexplainable.

In our first chapter on this subject, we made this statement: "Christian men seldom fall into this heresy while Christian, or, falling into it, are seldom Christian after it." And the argument we then used is abundantly sustained by the Word of God. Saul never thought of going to the witch for consultation until his sins had led him away from God, and his fear for the future drove him to confer with the demon's spirit that possessed her. Other cases might be given, full as pointed; but we have extended this chapter already beyond intended limits. And it will be conceded by all—but spiritualists—that spiritualism, being Antichrist, will not be, never has been, indulged in by Christians, until after they have forfeited the favor of God, and have ceased to be Christian.

And now we beg of all Christians, as did St. Paul, "Beloved, believe not every spirit, but try the spirits whether they be of God." "Jesus I know, and Paul I know; but who are ye?"

V.

SPIRITUALISM AND ANTICHRIST.

"But if our Gospel be hid, it is hid to them that are lost: in whom the god of this world hath blinded the minds of them which believe not."—2 COR. IV, 3, 4.

ALL Protestant writers, so far as we know, interpret Antichrist, or "the Man of Sin," as signifying Popery, or Romanism. And now, if we dissent, we are aware that we at once become subject to the charge of most flagrant heretical notions. But, after the most careful study of which we are capable, we are convinced it would be just as reasonable to interpret the Koran as the foundation of Mormonism; for, to our mind, there is no foundation in truth for any such exposition, only as it may be applied to Romanism as to the heresies of any other system of errors. The great measuring of swords that has been going on between Protestants and Catholics for many years, on this basis of conflict, is the veriest folly. We also take occasion to say, in this place, that the great phantom of "political Romanism," that has been so dexterously and zealously paraded before the American people for half a century, as if it were the only form of diabolical hatefulness that was worthy of the steel of the earnest Protestant polemic, has, in our judgment, but shown the shortsightedness of the zealot. We are aware that we are differing, now, from the popular idea of Protestant thinkers and writers on this important subject; for they interpret the "Man of Sin," with admirable unanimity, to mean the Pope of Rome. Our reasons for dissent shall be apparent hereafter.

It is just now popular with this class of writers to predict the great battle of God, the war of the spirits, the fight between Gog and Magog, speedily to take place on this proud

American Continent; and some possess enough of the prophet's ken—we had almost said are foolhardy enough—to locate the center of conflict in the Mississippi Valley. But the years go by, and the conflict is not apparent; or, certainly, not more so than it was three centuries ago.

If it were possible for the Gospel polemic to lay aside his theological lens, and adjust the non-partisan glasses of the statesman, and then retrospect this great but new nation, he would discover other elements of danger as potent as that of Romanism; and, indeed, would see in Romanism elements of danger only as they are apparent in any corrupt and fallen Church, cursed with devilish and inordinate greed for gain and worldly glory; for such Church, corrupted by demons and wholly destitute of the spirit of Christ, will not hesitate to use all means, fair or foul, for the accomplishment of its aims, on the plea of devils, that the end justifies the means. Such

Church is dangerous to the life of the nation, because its lust for power and wealth would unite Church and State. But, in this sense, the Catholic Church is not a particle in advance of the Protestant Episcopal Church, only as it has advantage in numbers. But who—unless it be the persecuted Cheney, of Chicago—would think of designating Bishop Whitehouse "the Man of Sin," or the Protestant Episcopal Church "the mystery of iniquity!" Yet there is as much authority, and as good Scriptural warrant for it, when Antichrist is properly understood, as there is for heaping unqualified epithets upon the Catholic Church, or for interpreting "the Man of Sin" as the Pope of Rome.

We do not thrust ourself forward as an apologist for Rome, nor for the Catholic Church; but we must protest against charging an offense upon a people who are just about as corrupt as Satan can make them, of which they are not guilty, any more than are

Protestant organizations who have departed from the true faith of the Gospel of Jesus, and who practice the corruptions of depravity, and who advocate the doctrine of demons. And all these we find in many factions and sects, but in none more than the one which goes by the name of spiritualism; for this one pre-eminently practices the doctrines of devils, with scarce an admixture of Gospel truth.

In the early ages of Christianity, the manifestations of a personal Antichrist were as confidently looked for as was the second coming of Christ. Irenæus, who had been instructed by the disciples of John, Papias, and Polycarp, asserts that Antichrist is the designation of an individual whom Satan shall use as his instrument to deceive those who dwell on the earth, for three years and a half; and that this false prophet, in support of his impious claims, shall work miracles; and, at last, the usurper shall be destroyed by the return of Christ to the earth. Now, while we would not rely wholly upon Irenæus in support of a Bible doctrine, yet this, we think, may be taken as proof of the prevailing opinions of those early days about the great Antichrist: First, that he should come, as some very wicked person; second, that he should rule, supreme, for a short time; and, third, that after his short but terrible reign, Christ should return and establish his own everlasting kingdom, to the utter destruction of "the Man of Sin," or of Antichrist.

But, before this occurs, the Jews are to be restored to Palestine—mark, not converted to Christ, but restored in unbelief—and shall, at the coming of Antichrist, possess Palestine as an independent state. This must be plain, because it is during this Jewish prosperity that Antichrist shall appear. And, according to the prediction of our Lord, the authority of Antichrist will then be acknowledged by the whole Jewish nation: "I am come in my

Father's name, and ye receive me not. When another shall come in his own name, him will ye receive."

The Lord Jesus, and the apostles too, plainly predict the apostasy of Christendom, and describe their corruptions as waxing worse and worse, until, like the Jews before them, in the abuse of God's goodness, his judgments overtake them, and they are cut off. In the present condition of the general Church of Christ, we can plainly trace the fulfillment of these predictions; for, though it be true there is real piety, and much vital godliness, in many branches of the true Church of Christ, yet, it is an alarming fact, "the mystery of iniquity doth already work," and the leaven of corruption hath already pervaded much of the mass. For this and many other generations, this leaven of unrighteousness may be partially stayed by the full and earnest consecration of heart and life to the service of Christ, by those who love our Lord Jesus in faith and sincerity. But the destiny of the mystery is to reach its climax in "that Wicked One."

However much the Popes of Rome have exalted themselves before men, and however arrogantly they have assumed the prerogatives of God, it can not be said of them they sit in the temple of God ; nor that they show themselves God, and demand the worship that should be given to God. Not even Pope Pius the Ninth, with the devilish infallibility dogma to back him, dares claim divine worship; but Antichrist shall exalt himself above all that is called God. How, then, can he be the Catholic Pope of Rome?

We are in the habit, as Protestants—and, for aught we know, Catholics do the same thing—of interpreting the wonderful vision of Nebuchadnezzar as a symbol of the kingdom of God, which shall break in pieces and destroy all other kingdoms. The stone cut out without hands, which crushed and destroyed the great image, we interpret as the Gospel of Christ, or the Christian Church; and the image, that is crushed and destroyed by this stone, we, as Protestants, interpret to be the Catholic Church. And, in turn, Catholicism interprets this same image as the foul heresy of Protestantism; and this, with them, is Antichrist. That both are in error, we think is evident, because of the character of the image, and also of the stone. The image represents the succession of four monarchies: the Babylonian was succeeded by the Medo-Persian; it by the Grecian; and the Grecian by the Roman. This great image was finally destroyed with the stroke of a stone; and, after this destruction of the image, the stone filled the whole earth.

Now, on the supposition that this image is "the Man of Sin," and that Christianity is to overthrow it, we must note two things about the stone: First, it was cut out without hands, thus precluding the possibility of all human agency in its formation, while it is claimed by all Christians that human agency and human instrumentality are distinguishing features of the Christian dispensation; but, second, the stone did not expand until after the image was wholly destroyed. Christianity has expanded a millionfold, but "the Man of Sin" is not crushed. We may add one other thought about the stone. It did not change the character of the image, but with fury destroyed it; whereas, the great aim of Christianity is to convert and save.

But, by applying the image to the Catholic Church, we involve ourselves in yet greater difficulty; because, first, in the king's vision the stone came in contact with the image after the division of the Roman Empire; whereas, Christianity came in contact with the Empire while it was at its greatest glory and in its strongest unity. Moreover, though the Roman empire has been overthrown, it did not fall by Christianity, but by barbarians.

Then, it follows, both the stroke of the stone and the destruction of the image are yet in the future. And since the kingdom of Christ is already reaching out to fill the world, we can not conclude that the stone of Nebuchadnezzar's dream represents it; and, since Catholicism is not crushed, but is in great power, that it was symbolized, by the great image, as "the Man of Sin."

But now, while we have assumed—and, we think, maintained—that Antichrist is not Catholicism, and that the image of the beast is not the Pope of Rome, but is a great and powerful wicked monster of a man that is yet to come, we are ready now to take ground definitely—as we have already implied—that Antichrist, in substance and principle, is manifest in all the workings of Satan among men. Especially is the spirit of Antichrist seen in the workings of Satan, developed in all heresies and false doctrines.

It is the prerogative of God to forgive sin,

and he alone hath power to do so; for he alone hath the words of eternal life. But Catholicism grants absolution, grants indulgences, curses and blesses her votaries at pleasure; and this is Antichrist.

Again: it is the prerogative of the Lord Jesus to make intercession for sinners; for, "if any man sin, we have an advocate with the Father, even Jesus Christ the righteous." Catholicism substitutes the intercessions of the priesthood, of fallible men, for that of Jesus. It will not be denied that few of the rank and file—the membership—of the Catholic Church ever pray to God the Father, through Jesus, his Son. And this is the spirit of Antichrist.

Again: the Lord God is supreme. "Thou shalt worship the Lord thy God, and him only shalt thou serve;" but Catholics worship the Host, and pray to the Virgin. And this, too, is the spirit of Antichrist.

But are there no other forms of heresy that

partake of the spirit of Antichrist, by perverting the Word of God and substituting the doctrine of demons?

David says, "The law of the Lord is perfect, converting the soul;" but infidelity and and spiritualism reject the law of the Lord as it reveals the plan of life and salvation through Jesus Christ, and substitutes the dim readings of nature, and the dark, bungling, contradictory revelations of demons, through a human medium. And this is the spirit of "that Wicked One," "the Man of sin."

Or, again, God's Word very plainly puts a difference, in time, between him that serveth God and him that serveth him not; and, for the spirit-life, God has very plainly defined the abode of both good and bad. But spiritualism, for the life that now is, sets aside the Word of God for the indulgence of the grossest vice, and receives the communication of demons concerning the future state; while the infidel sneers at the idea of sin in this life, assuming there is no Supreme Being to be sinned against, and for the spirit-life he feels contempt. Both, in their way, are found fighting against God. And this is plainly the spirit of that Antichrist. And thus they are lost to the power of the Gospel of Jesus; for they, being blinded by the god of this world, follow his devices, and are led captive by him at his will, beyond the reach of the light of the Gospel.

There is about as much hope of a demon's redemption as there is of the final salvation of a confirmed infidel or of a full-fledged spiritualist, they being fully given over to reprobacy of mind, to believe a lie that they may be damned. The Gospel is hid to them. "But if our Gospel be hid, it is hid to them that are lost: in whom the god of this world hath blinded the minds of them which believe not."

VI.

DECEPTION OF SPIRITUALISM.

"It shall even be as when a hungry man dreameth, and, behold, he eateth; but he awaketh, and his soul is empty."
ISAIAH XXIX, 8.

"But the multitude of the proud shall be like the small dust; And like the flitting chaff, the multitude of the terrible."
BISHOP LOWTH.

SOLOMON said, "There is a way that seemeth right unto a man; but the end thereof is the way of death." The cunning of the adversary of our race is evidenced in his gilding the pathway to ruin, so that it seems more pleasant and attractive to the traveler's eye than all others. The ability manifest in this will be apparent, when we consider that directly the reverse is true. The way of holiness is a highway; a narrow way, strait and clean; a pleasant way, full of grandest mountain scenery; a bountiful pathway, hanging full of the richest clusters of grapes on every hand. Yea, it is crowded with all manner of richness and good things, exactly suited to the want and taste of the immortal spirit of the traveler. But, with all this, its pleasure can only be enjoyed, and its richness possessed, by such as walk in the path; and the beautiful scenery can only be discerned by those whose feet press the heavenly road, and whose spiritual eyes look out from Pisgah's top into the valley of Eshcol. Because of this, poor benighted wayfarers look in vain for the beauty of the way. And, moreover, the prince of darkness has so beclouded the mental vision of the wayfarer, that he not only sees no beauty in the path of life, but to him it seems, of all other ways, the most gloomy; for Satan hath blinded his eyes. But what is more strange than all this is, the pathway of sin is broad and ugly, full of the foulest things outside of perdition, and the worst possible company crowd the road horribly. The drunkard and the thief, the liar, the whoremonger, the harlot, and the churl, the blasphemer, the murderer, the gambler, and the infidel, are all on this road.

The road itself is horrible. Quagmires, deep, dark, and dangerous pitfalls, are yawning all the length of it. And, besides, it is but a short journey on it until the traveler finds himself smothering in the slough of despond, which dangerous lagoon stretches clear across the way. And yet this terrible road seems the right one to multitudes, who do not realize that the end is death.

Satan is ever industriously employed in strewing the way with such seductive pleasures as will most likely delude the sense and deceive the eye. And by this means he gilds the pleasures of sin with an attractive charm, which so entrances the giddy pleasure-seeker that Satan can readily convince him that any thing so pleasant must be innocent and harmless; and, if harmless, then it must be right. Once settled in this, he will not only indulge in the practice, but will quite earnestly defend the sin. This is but a natural process.

Take, as a sample in proof of this, the lover of strong drink. No sober man will advocate intoxication, But men have drunk to excess, and defended the right, for many generations; because, first, they have tasted the dangerous draft, and have been thrilled with the intoxication. True, there was the smiting of the conscience, and the sense of shame and degradation; but they have drunk, and drunk again, until, in self-defense, for protection from the stings of conscience and for a covering of their shame, they have hunted for arguments to prove the correctness of the hateful practice. These, by Satan's aid, they have soon found, and, finding them, they became confirmed drunkards. After this, all words of reason and argument are lost on them; for they are now fortified in their own ruin.

This might be illustrated in many ways. Men loving sin, and being naturally opposed to the law of the Lord, the common resort is, either to pervert the Word of God by false interpretation, or to deny it wholly. Of the latter class is the open infidel and the atheist, who, like David's fool, say in their hearts there is no God. But of the former is the heretical perverter of the Word of God, of every grade and order.

And chief among them all are the modern spiritualists. We say modern spiritualists, because the spiritualists of olden time made no claim to a belief in the law of God. And although it is true that very many of the modern spiritualist lecturers and writers deny God and revelation, yet many of them are avowed believers in the Scriptures of Divine truth. All these, assuming belief in God's Word, are yet not content with the revelation that it makes of the spirit-world; and rejecting the truth of its teaching, that no traveler to the bourne of the dead can ever return at the bidding of sinful mortals, they resort to the professed spiritual medium, allow themselves to listen to—ah! and to receive as worthy of credit—the contradictory and absurd telegrams of demons as authentic dispatches from their dear friends who inhabit the spirit-world. And, as marvelous as it seems to a believer in the plain Word of God, whose stamp of condemnation is upon all such unlawful means of obtaining intelligence from the spirit-world, this class of dreaming fanatics receive such reports of demons as more reasonable than Scriptural truth. They are as in a feverish dream, and suppose that they have intercourse with the dead. Some that we could name are so infatuated with this belief, that with them the control and care that the spirits have of the believer in their agency wholly supersedes the providence of God.

A lady, whose culture and refinement is acknowledged by those who know her—whose name we suppress—is in possession of a very pretty home in the most aristocratic part of the city, and has, in connection with her residence, a very great variety of flowers. These flowers, in their season, show remarkable thrift and care in their resplendent bloom. This lady matron, who is an avowed and somewhat noted spiritualist medium, on being asked by a lady friend, who was delighted with the beauty of the flowers, how she managed to have such great success in floral culture, gravely responded:

"Ah, my dear! the work is nothing. I give myself no concern about the flowers. I trust their keeping wholly to the spirits. They do it all. I have only to be careful to leave a bucket of water where they can get it every night—for they are fond of water—and all the rest they do for me."

Now, dear reader, do you smile at such

presumption? So did we when we first learned of the incident; but, we can assure you, no full-fledged spiritualist will think of criticising such confidence in the watch-care of the spirits.

This same lady is in the habit of placing plate and chair at the table at each meal, where a daughter—long since deceased—was wont to sit during her life-time. And this she does in full confidence that the spirit of the daughter is present at the table of her mother, each day, for her daily bread. Is the mother foolish? Yes: there is no question of that with sane people. But the proof is not wanting that hundreds of spiritualists are equally foolish; though most of them exhibit the insanity of the blind stupor in a different way. For all of them, in the very act of receiving spiritualism, discredit the Scriptures, provoke Jehovah, and offer an insult to the intelligence of man. But "as a hungry man dreameth, and, behold, he eateth," but, alas! there must be an awakening; "and when he awaketh his soul hath appetite."

Solomon says, "Know thou that for all these things God will bring thee into judgment." "Then," says Malachi, "shall ye return, and discern between the righteous and the wicked, between him that serveth God and him that serveth him not."

These foolish and wicked triflings, this presumptuous setting at naught of the plain Word of God, may endure for a time; yea, the cunning, crafty perverter of the Scriptures may hold blindly on to his delusion during his natural life-time; but there cometh a day of awakening, a day of arousing up from the delusive dream. And then, alas! though in the terribly delusive dream the appetite was, or seemed to be, sated, yet now, at the wakening, "the soul hath appetite;" that is, the soul is not satisfied, the intellectual being is disappointed. As the wrecked mariner, cast on desert shore, naked, thirsty, famishing with hunger, falls into troubled slumber, he dreams, and in the vision he is again at home, surrounded by all that heart could wish; he and his friends gather around the festal board; they eat, drink, and are merry; the feast is of most prodigal provision—all have eaten to the full; but "he awaketh and his soul hath appetite." Then is the desolation and destitution of the poor mariner doubly terrible.

We are sad with our reflections when we remember there are thousands of dreaming immortals, cast on the sterile reef of spiritualism, slumbering away in the fateful dream of the carnally secure, refusing to be wakened because the illusive spell of demons is upon them; and, with dogged persistence, continue to build their hopes of a blissful immortality on this foundation of demoniacal possession.

But both the faith and practice of men is to be finally tested; and, doubtless, to this testing the apostle refers, in the third chapter of 1 Corinthians, when he says, "For other foundation can no man lay than that is laid, which is Jesus Christ. Now, if any man build upon this foundation, gold, silver, precious stones, wood, hay, stubble, every man's work shall be made manifest; for the day shall declare it, because it shall be revealed by fire; and the fire shall try every man's work, of what sort it is."

Men can go through the world with any heresy, their love of carnal pleasure lifting them above the fear of consequences. And often not until the final hour of life do they awake to the terrible delusive dream. Then the bitterness of death is doubly bitter. But awake from the stupor of heresy men must, and that, too, unexpectedly, suddenly.

Jesus said, "In an hour that ye think not the Son of man cometh;" and the Lord God has said, "I will laugh at your calamities, when your fear cometh as desolation."

In closing this chapter, we earnestly but

kindly ask all intelligent spiritualists if an instance can be given where the believer in spiritualism triumphed over the fear of death, with an intelligent triumph. Such information, from reliable source, might modify our horror of the monstrous heresy.

St. Paul said, "The sting of death is sin, the strength of sin is the law; but thanks be unto God, who giveth us the victory through our Lord Jesus Christ."

Multitudes have in all ages believed this; and, going to God in the name of Jesus Christ, have passed from under the ban of the law, and have been enabled to triumph, through Jesus, over the last enemy, which is death. Paul, addressing those of this faith, said, in holy exultation, "This is the victory that overcometh the world, even our faith."

Compared with this holy, triumphant expectancy, the vague, unsatisfying contradictions of spiritualism are as the blackness of darkness, even for this life. But for the death-hour, and the life to come, there is no word in the English language that is bold enough to show the contrast between him who, in full confidence of the truth of revelation, meets the final foe, and, in the strength that Jesus gives, passes over into the land of the blessed, and him who, in life, substituted for the Word of God the confusing and uncertain revelations of the spiritual *seance*.

The servant of God, in such hour, exclaims, "I know that my Redeemer liveth," and shouts, with David of old, "Though I walk through the valley and shadow of death, I will fear no evil;" or, with Paul, he will shout the victory in words like these: "For we know that if our earthly house of this tabernacle were dissolved, we have a building of God, a house not made with hands, eternal in the heavens."

Now, what is the language of the spiritualist in the trying hour? Ah! what? Let the dumb, confused stupor of such, in the terrible trial, show to all living the dangerous deception of the frightful heresy; for it is the delusion of demons seeking the ruin of souls.

VII.

SPIRIT OF INQUIRY IN MAN; OR, THE OFFICE OF PHILOSOPHY.

"Ever learning, and never able to come to the knowledge of the truth."—2 TIM. III, 7.

"For as I passed by, and beheld your devotions, I found an altar with this inscription, TO THE UNKNOWN GOD. Whom therefore ye ignorantly worship, him declare I unto you."—ACTS XVII, 23.

A CHEMICAL test, dropped into a quiescent mass, will effect a combination of new affinities; but, before such affinities are formed, there must be first a separation of elements, an active effervesence, then the combination.

This may illustrate what is going on continually in human Society. Events occur, questions arise, which compel the separation of opinions, and the passing over to opposite poles of antagonistic forces.

Before the chemical test, the old mass seemed to be in harmonious rest. So, where no test question of Divine truth assails the moral quiet of the unregenerate, there is the quiet of the grave. But since the entrance of sin into the world, there has been the disturbing element; for righteousness and sin can never live in harmony. These are the antagonistic forces, out of which must come the new affinities and the final harmony. But as the forces are opposing, there must be, during the formatory stage, much disquiet.

The Gospel of Jesus Christ falls upon the moral mass of our race much as the chemical test. But men have volition; and though disturbed, yet, loving the old element of sin, they "do always resist the Holy Ghost." And yet, being once disturbed, our race has never been able to find quiet while resisting the truth of the Gospel.

This may, in part, account for the many devices of men looking after rest for the disturbed quiet of the heart. The struggle is no new one, only it develops in different forms in almost every age, it being the evident practice of Satan, when beaten at one point, to concentrate his forces on another, ever counting it victory so long as he can keep men from finding the true God, from whom man is estranged. The Lord has largely defeated him in this, by planting in man a desire to find his way back to God, and by holding out to his stumbling feet lanterns for the pathway, in the heavens above and in the earth beneath, all seeming to say, Come back to God, come back to God! To the myriad beckoning hands in nature, God has added all truth, in morals and science, to aid benighted man in his search for the living God; for it is evident that the tendency of all true science is to the acknowledgment of the true God of heaven and earth.

Dr. Cocker has plainly shown, in his "Greek Philosophy," that even the Greeks were very largely indebted to Hebrew religion for their philosophy. Christianity, it is true, in the third and fifth centuries, became somewhat imbued with the Platonic school of Greece; yet the philosophy of the Greeks imbibed a religious hue from the Christianity of the Hebrew.

That the Greeks were not aware of the former, nor the Christians of the latter, does not disparage the fact, nor disprove the assumption. Nor yet is it a marvel; for only in the light of developed ages do we read clearly the pages of the past.

The millions of to-day read as blindly the printing of the every-day page of history as did the Athenians in Paul's day bow to the unknown god whom they ignorantly worshiped. But the student of to-day, aided by the light of reason, science, and revelation—standing with Paul, on Mars' Hill, at Athens, surrounded by the temples, statues, and altars which Grecian art had consecrated to pagan worship—would read, with the enthusiasm of the Christian philosopher and scientist, the unseen hand of Deity, guiding, in all this sculptured grandeur, and controlling, in all the mazes of their confused wisdom, to the one uncontrollable, resultant development of the unknown God, so boldly declared unto them by St. Paul.

To the Christian student, it is a pleasing reflection God's revelation of himself is as positively and—to him—as plainly recorded in the Book of Nature as in the Book of Revelation, or the Bible; for it may be readily shown that, while the rejector of the Bible, and those ignorant of the Scriptural revelations of Deity, fail to find God in nature, yet the legitimate tendency of the diligent study of nature, guided by reason alone—which, when enlightened, always demands cause for effect—is the development of the Supreme, or great First Cause. Nor have the efforts of infidels been able to show the contrary, in this or any other age; though the most scientific analyses of the germinal properties of life have been invoked by Darwin and others.

For what does all the learned research of those able and scholarly naturalists show, if it be not the necessity of some great First Cause for all things? True, they have gone into the secret and labyrinthian mazes of the hitherto undiscovered germinal properties of life, or protoplasm; but beyond this, while they reject the Bible, they can not go—and so have stood, and must forever stand, confounded by their own wonderful discoveries. As with the ancient skeptic naturalist, so with the modern, each arriving in his turn at the limit of his power in research.

But no such altar and inscription would have been erected and inscribed as Paul saw at Athens, had not the philosophy of the Greeks constantly led them on to the discovery of the "unknown God, whom they ignorantly worshiped."

Our convictions of the sequel of unfinished explorations in the field of science, must, of course, be founded upon the results of the past research of the scientist. And by this rule we see, first, the unsatisfied longing of the mind of each philosopher for yet greater discoveries, even after the rules of his craft are fully exhausted; and, second, that the ever-restless spirit within him urges him on to such efforts of discovery as will lead to the attainment of the end.

And as correct rules in philosophy must lead to the solution of all philosophical problems, so the legitimate tendency of the philosophical research of the ancients was to lead them through nature up to nature's God. And if it be asked, If modern theorists fail to find the true God, and even hold the existence of Deity as doubtful, then can it be inferred that the ancient philosopher would ever, unaided, have gained a knowledge of the unknown God? we answer, Knowledge is not intuitive, but a desire for knowledge is; or, at least, man is not wanting in an internal incentive to the acquisition of knowledge.

Assuming, with Job, "There is a spirit within man, and the inspiration of the Almighty giveth him understanding," and if, when correct geometrical rules are observed, then the most difficult problems in geometry are solved, does it not follow that the philosophical research of the ancients, which led, even in the first years of Christianity, to the acknowledgment of the existence of the unknown God, in ideal, have led them—possibly—in other generations, to grasp the reality of such being, made, in nature, manifest and known?

But if it be objected such assumption argues against the necessity of Divine revelation, we answer, This was the time of "the fullness of the Gentiles," and Christ, the hitherto unknown, must now be manifest unto Greek as well as unto Jew. And while the Jew, by aid of the Divine prediction of his coming in prophecy, could readily receive him through penitence and faith as the Christ, "the sent of God," so the learned Greek, whose philosophy had led him no farther than the ideal unknown, would be able, by adding to his philosophy the revelations of the New Testament Scriptures, to receive him whom Paul so eloquently declared unto them.

But if, again, it be urged that the modern scientist is as far from a knowledge of the true God as were the ancients, we again answer, the tendency of all true science is to the discovery of first or elementary cause, which is the self-existent. And it is known to every student that the speculative vagaries of the ancients will not compare with the more reasonable productions of such men as Rénan, Darwin, Huxley, or even Owen.

So far as we know, all modern, rationalistic,

material theorists allow primal cause for all things, stumbling only on the nature and character of such primal cause. A learned author, from whom we have already quoted, says, "Science is inevitably approaching the idea that all kinds of force are but forms or manifestations of some one central force, issuing from some one fountain-head of power." Modern writers, of nearly all classes, acknowledge the form of force, which is a type of all the rest, is consciousness of living effort in volition. All force, then, is of one type, and that type is mind. In its last analysis, external causation may be resolved into Divine energy. The great astronomer, Herschel, says, "The force of gravitation is the direct result of a consciousness, or will, exerted somewhere."

And now, if this conclusion results from a scientific study of the heavens, without the aid of revelation, may not the humble Christian, with the revelation of Jesus Christ, heartily exclaim, "Power belongs to God?" And is he not justified in believing that it is through Divine energy that all things are, and are upheld; and that in God we live and move and have our being?

Those who resign the government of this world to Satan, may see nothing in the philosophy of the ancients but a simple creation of Satan; but he who believes that the entire control and progress of humanity is in the hand of a merciful Providence, must see that, in the purposes of God, even ethnicism has fulfilled some end, and that heathenism has at least shown the want, and to some extent prepared the mind for the advent, of Christianity; for, it must be noted, God has never left himself without a witness, in any nation. True, the religion of the Athenians was not able to release them from the guilt of sin, nor redeem them from its power or make them pure and holy; and thus, practically, it brought them no nearer to God. But it did awaken in them a conscience, and educate it; and it developed in them more fully the sense of sin and guilt, and made them conscious of their inability to save themselves. And thus it created in them a felt want of something more than mere embellishment and culture; and, the moment such sense is aroused, man sees the importance and feels the need of being saved from the consequences of sin by a higher power.

Æsthetic taste had found, in Athens, full gratification. Poetry, sculpture, architecture, were all brought to the highest perfection; but the need of something higher, deeper, and more true, was not only felt, but was written on the very stones; so that, while the solid granite grandly expressed the flashing power of their genius, it also held in ineffaceable grasp the wailings of the prompter of that genius—the wailings of an unsatisfied soul. To fill this void, or to satisfy this hunger, they erected an altar to the unknown

God, and ignorantly worshiped him. They had lords many, and gods many; but, in the erection of this altar, they confessed a felt want of something higher than all these.

The strength and weakness of heathen mythology consisted in the contradictory character of their deities; for through it all there is a blending of the natural and the supernatural, the human and the Divine. Zeus, the eternal king, the immortal ruler, whose will is ever sovereign, has something of human weakness. God and man are thus in some mysterious way united. And may we not consider this as in evidence of the deepest longing of the human heart—that is, an unconquerable desire to bring God nearer to the human apprehension and closer to the human heart? Hence, also, the hold paganism had, in Paul's day, upon the Grecian mind.

But in this human aspect was also found its weakness; for, when philosophic thought is brought into contact with and permitted critically to test mythology, it dethrones its false gods.

The age of spontaneous religious sentiments must be succeeded by the age of reflection. Popular theological faith must be put into the crucible of dialectic analysis, that the frivolous and the false may be taken from the pure and the true. For the reason of man must be as well satisfied as his heart; and faith in God must have a logical basis. It must be founded on demonstration and truth, and the question, Is God cognizable by the human mind? must be reasonably answered. And if this can be achieved, then a deeper foundation is laid in the mind of humanity, upon which Christianity can rear her higher and nobler truths. And by this rule of philosophy Paul declared, "That which can be known of God is manifested in their hearts, God himself having shown it to them;" and with such thought he proceeded to say, "As I passed by and beheld your sacred objects, I found an altar with this inscription upon it, To the unknown God."

This idea of a God who is the unconditioned cause of all things, may have been possessed, unacknowledged, by Paul's auditors; yet, doubtless, it was in consequence of his discovery of this fundamental principle of all religion, that emboldened him so eloquently to declare the true God, in the midst of so much idolatry. We infer this; for a mere blind impulse never guides man to the true end of his being. A simple tendency to the perfection of his nature, without a revealed object, would be but mockery and misery—an *ignis-fatuus*, perpetually alluring, but always deceiving him.

The idea of God is revealed to man in the spontaneous development of his intelligence. And the existence of a supreme reality, corresponding to and represented by this idea, is rationally and logically demonstrable, and therefore justly entitled to take rank as part of our legitimate, valid, and positive knowledge.

But it must not be supposed that such conclusions were reached more frequently by philosophers of Paul's day than by the mere scientist of the present time; for many of them, as is the scientist of the present day, were in the habit of resolving all substances into self-existent being, simply upon the hypothesis that all knowledge is limited to material phenomena; that is, to appearances perceptible to human sense. Thus, we can not know the essence of any object, nor the real mode of procedure of any event; but simply its relation to other events, as similar or dissimilar, coexistent or successive; and these always the same.

The constant resemblances which link phenomena together, and the constant sequences which unite them as antecedent and consequent, are, by this class of naturalists, termed laws; while they acknowledge that their nature and anterior causes are to them wholly unknown.

But, on the other hand, the philosophical analysis of Plato, and many others of his school, lead constantly to the revelation of real cause and being.

We are wont to condemn, without charity, the sculptured grandeur of Athens, the Temple of Diana, together with the Altar of the Unknown God, as being but the impulse of a wicked and idolatrous race of sensual materialists; but the student of nature and revelation will not fail to see the goodness and providential care of God in all this restlessness of the ancient thinker, as he in nature and art sought for a satisfying portion. For it is now evident that God gave to this unrest a preparatory place and office, which, if it did not bring them to a full knowledge of the truth, nevertheless prepared their minds for the full investigation of Paul's declaration of the unknown God. This is shown in the awakening and enthronement of conscience as a law of duty; and also in exhibiting to the awakened conscience the great distance and estrangement from God, showing the need of a mediator between man and God, who, unlike the Grecian image in sculptured granite, must not stand stolid and mute before the penitent worshiper; but who would lay hold of the man, and plead with God, thus insuring reconciliation.

Thus God has ever used the quickened thought of the ages to prepare the mind, and turn the masses to himself for safety and rest.

Let the Christian, then, instead of cowardly yielding the field of science to the skeptic, take courage. God has not left mankind in hopeless unrest; and we apprehend that the present attacks of the materialist and scientist will not only come to naught while they try vainly to pull down the Christian's tower of strength, but it will be seen ultimately to redound to the glory of God and the firmer upbuilding of the cause of Christ. For, as the ancients were "ever learning," and were not able to come to a knowledge of the truth until they unconsciously acknowledged the failure of their philosophy to bring peace to the heart of unrest, in the erection of the Altar to the Unknown God, so the physiologist of modern day, in his vain endeavor to reject God, has been, by the unfailing correctness of his own philosophy, led to confess the limit of his own powers, and to the acknowledgment of some greater power beyond. This is shown in the fact that, no sooner has one scientist discovered and made known to the restless world of skeptics the wonderful protoplasm, or the germinal properties of life, than a hundred voices demand the origin of the protoplasm itself, not knowing that, in doing this, all the truth of God's Word becomes proved, and Christianity established.

Let the skeptic go on with his skepticism;

let the scientist continue his scientific research,—they will but show him the weakness of man, and develop the power of God. And may the great Eternal Spirit hasten the day when the "Unknown God" shall be declared unto all nations, and the name of Jesus be sung, in every land by every tongue! Amen.

VIII.

A WORD TO SPIRITUALISTS.

"Now the Spirit speaketh expressly, that in the latter times some shall depart from the faith, giving heed to seducing spirits, and doctrines of devils."—I TIM. IV, I.

NO student, either of the Word of God or the book of nature, will charge God with redundancy, or with the performance of an unnecessary thing. For the complete production of all things in nature, he gave but one command to each; and, in perfect order and harmony, they sprang into being— the light, the earth, the sea, the fish, the fowl, the beast, the sun for the day, and the moon and the stars for the night.

But one command in prohibition to the federal head, and but one penalty was affixed to its violation. And after the pitiful fall, but one promise of man's redemption was given by the Almighty Father. At the fullness of time, but one Savior came into the world for the redemption of the one pledge, that the seed of the woman should bruise the serpent's head. True, the prophets grew eloquent, and their messages ever and anon thrilled the generations of the long-rolling ages, as the Holy Ghost revealed to them the coming Messiah; but all the hallowed fire of their glowing tongues ever glowed around the one promise of his coming.

One voice at the Jordan, when Jesus was baptized, cried out from earth, "Behold the Lamb of God;" and one from heaven thrilled the astonished multitude with the one exclamation, "This is my beloved Son, in whom I am well pleased: hear ye him." And but one dove descended and alighted upon Jesus, thus testifying to his Divine Sonship. Twelve legions of angels were ready to testify for Jesus; but with this announcement of his Divinity, he went forth on his Divine mission.

He mingled freely, as a man, with the apostles; but he showed himself but once during his sojourn with them in transfiguration. He was but once in an agony, in the Garden. He bore but one cross for us. He was crucified once, for all. He was dead, and buried, but one time; but that once was all-sufficient; for he conquered the monster foe, hell, for a time. He burst the bonds of death, and came forth in glorious triumph, giving to earth this immortal assurance: Death and the grave have no power that Jesus can not break. Once more he ascended on high—once for all—where he ever liveth to make intercession for all that love him.

From these facts, we may learn the great God never uses unnecessary means for the accomplishment of any work for man, or for any created intelligence. To Satan, who said to him, "If thou be the Son of God, command that these stones be made bread," Jesus answered, "Man shall not live by bread alone." And again, when the tempter tried him from another stand-point, he did not enter into lengthened argument, but simply said, "It is written, Thou shalt not tempt the Lord thy God." To the caviling Pharisees, he said: "This is an evil generation. They seek a sign, and there shall no sign be given it but the sign of Jonas the prophet." To the anxious and troubled soul of Dives he answered, "Neither would they be persuaded though one arose from the dead."

The lesson to us is this: God has, by the inspiration of his Spirit, caused to be recorded in his Word all that we need know, in life, to secure our happiness here, and our safety and joy forever.

"Of making many books there is no end;" but there is but one Bible. God has faithfully and plainly recorded himself in one volume; and O, what a volume it is!—as high as the heavens, as deep as infinity. No marvel that groveling, sensual minds stagger at its mysteries. But it has this astonishing peculiarity: the simple-minded may grasp enough of its truth to be guided into the way of life forever; but, alas! with the blinding clouds of doubt and distrust that Satan is ever throwing about the human mind, we stumble at the plainest truth it records.

It is, happily, the province of the Christian to believe God, as he talks through his Word; and, believing his Word, to know Jesus whom he hath sent. And with this confidence and knowledge, he is fortified against the tempter's startling suggestions about the future state; for the Jesus in whom he trusts has said to him, through his Word, "I go to prepare a place for you, that where I am there ye may be also." In this he trustingly and calmly rests his soul, and, with the psalmist, exclaims, "Though I walk through the valley of the shadow of death, I will fear no evil; for thou art with me, thy rod and thy staff they comfort me;" or with Paul, the trusting man of God, can say joyfully, "To live is Christ, but to die is gain."

Not so with the doubting distruster of God's Word. To him, life is all full of perplexity, the grave is dismal, and eternity is dreadful. To him it is a terribly long time since Jesus was here among men; and, to his restless mind, the record that God made of himself, by the hand of Moses, of the beginning of time and the creation of all terrestrial things, seems so far in the distant past that a hungry longing springs up in his soul for some fresh revelation of God and the spirit-interests of man. And then, losing sight of the revelations already made, that one day with the infinite God is as a thousand years and a thousand years as one day, and that Jesus Christ is the same yesterday, to-day, and forever, without variableness or shadow of turning; and forgetting that if such an unchangeable God, who has all power, declared, eighteen hundred years ago—by man's count—that he was going to prepare a place for his servants that day, then such place is prepared this day for all that love him; but, though the Bible has faithfully given warning, and "the Spirit has spoken expressly that in the latter times some shall depart from the faith, giving heed to seducing spirits and doctrines of devils," yet multitudes, in their blindness, ignore or reject all this, and do give heed to seducing spirits and doctrines of devils. For what but this can induce men to close their eyes to the fact that God in his Word has revealed to man all that he ought to know, in this life, of the spirit-life to come, and, turning away from revelation, betake them to the contradictory uncertainties of the spiritual medium, in dark *seance?* If it were nothing worse to do so, it would show very great distrust in and dissatisfaction with the revelations God has been pleased to make, to the citizens of earth, about the ample provision he has made for all who serve him.

But the resort of the spiritualist for intelligence from the spirit-world not only discredits God, but it credits and propagates the falsehoods of demons. Having departed from the faith, they give heed to seducing spirits and doctrines of devils. Mark: those spirits are seducing. To seduce, is to draw aside from the path of rectitude. And this is the office that is especially assigned to those malignant demons who lead poor mortals away from God, until they deny the faith. Then they are ready to heed also the doctrines of devils.

God has plainly told us, in his Word, of the abode of the spirits of the justified. The ever-memorable answer of Jesus, to the trusting penitent on the cross, is all-sufficient: "This day shalt thou be with me in paradise."

Stephen, also, when about to die, saw the gates of the spirit-home wide open, and the angels too, as they came fluttering down to the dying man, as if in a hurry to bear his spirit to the home of the soul. These, with kindred cases throughout the Scriptures, and in the experience of the Christian world, settle the safe abode of the spirits of all who trust in Jesus.

Necromancers, astrologers, and spiritual mediums have for many ages taken advantage of the seeming mystery that enshrouds the state of the dead, and have speculated upon the broken-hearted, bereaved friends of the departed; and have made both notoriety and money by pretending to receive important messages from the dead.

Christian reader, if it be true that the Word of God has not yet allayed the preying anxiety of your mind and heart about the safe abode and soul-security of wife or child or very dear friend, let us devote one moment, in the light of reason and common sense, to the candid investigation of the claims of spiritualists.

Let us enter the chamber of your beloved friend. That friend is a devout servant of God. The breathing is already short and hurried; the pulse is but a flutter. Life is certainly receding; for the pallor of death is on the brow. We are in deepest sympathy, and give utterance to our sorrow in a rain of tears. We watch with all eagerness every symptom of change. One step more, and our dear friend will be gone.

Mark the effort; our friend is struggling to speak. Do you hear that exclamation? It is with faltering lip, but it is the shout of the victor. If we heard them correctly, these were the words: "Thanks be unto God, who giveth us the victory through our Lord Jesus Christ!"

A moment more, and all is over. The body is dead. But where is the spirit? what is its state? and will it—can it—again answer my call? We try it; we call to it to come back; we shout aloud for but one more word,—but all is still as the grave.

Must we part forever? We go to the grave to weep and call. If we were listening, inspiration would answer: "Not here. Why seek ye the living among the dead?" But the deaf ear of our reason is stopped to this voice, and we turn away in dumb silence, with great sorrow.

Just now, spiritualism comes in, to take advantage of our sorrow and of our hungry longing to hear something of our dead. The mediums are the dupes of "seducing spirits," and they "give heed to doctrines of devils," or demons; and these demons pretend to answer the call of the medium, with some message from our friend.

Aside from revelation, two very important things make this pretense absurd:

First, our departed friend, while in life,

could not have been induced to associate, in any way whatever, with this vile nest of spiritualists who breed the doctrine of devils; for, throughout life, our loved one abominated the damnable heresy; and death produces no change morally. Hence the assumption of the medium, of a visit from such a one, is unreasonable.

But, second, on the supposition that it were possible for our friend to come back to earth for any purpose, would it not be more reasonable to suppose that the visit would be to friends, kindred, and loved ones, than to suppose our dearest, pure, loved one should seek out the dark, stealthy *seance*, where are met, for the orgies of demons, those whose morals are bad, and whose theories and practices are in flagrant violation of the laws and usages of all decency in civilized lands? Can any sane man conceive it a reasonable thing that a pure spirit, saved by the merit of the Lord Jesus, all clad in white robe, washed in the blood of the Lamb, should ever visit such assembly of demons, both spiritual and incarnate, as is usually found in the circle of spiritualists when convened for their nightly sessions? The very thought is revolting, and is the reverse of all that the Scriptures have taught us about the employment of the saints in light. "A man is known by the company he keeps." This will not be called in question in this world. Like seeks like; and it is a law of our being that we are unhappy if our associates be not congenial. Because of this, men choose their associates to correspond with their own tastes and morals. The Scriptures draw the same distinctive line for the spirit-life. And for the abode of the good there must be preparatory cleansing; for "nothing that is unclean, impure, or unholy can enter there." But for the abode of the wicked, all that is vile and impure shall enter it.

Now, with such marked difference, how

absurd to suppose the spirits of the justified ever appear to answer the call of a profligate medium in this world! We can conceive of no more monstrous villainy than to impose on the credulity of the bereaved and broken-hearted, by bringing pretended messages, received by spiritual mediums, to the sad and sorrow-stricken ones. And the atrocious diabolism is all the more hideous and hell-deserving when, as is usually the case, the forged message is in flagrant opposition to the whole life, faith, and practice of the departed.

Let Christians beware; for "the Spirit speaketh expressly that in the latter times some shall depart from the faith, giving heed to seducing spirits and doctrines of devils."

To those who have already fallen into this snare of Satan we have a word of counsel, and we are done.

And, first, we are ready to admit that many of you are sincere and honest in your convictions of the truth of what is called spiritualism; but you are the victims of the cunning of both bad men and devils. This we have plainly shown in these chapters. Satan, who is ever seeking to turn the mind of man away from God, was not slow in recognizing the earnest desire of humanity to peer into the mysterious abode of the dead, and to learn something more than is revealed in the Holy Scriptures of the employment of the spirits of our friends in the spirit-world. To the deception, he has from the first used a double agency; namely, wicked, deceitful men, and demons. These constitute every complete circle of spiritualists. These cunning demons, under the tuition of Satan, their chief, are masters in all jugglery, magic, and witchcraft; and, with bad men and women to help them, are able to make such demonstrations in the "dark sittings" of the circle as are calculated to deceive the credulous, unsuspecting victim.

Let me remind you of a fact, patent even to stanch spiritualists themselves, that should excite your alarm. The pretended revelations of the spirits are often flatly contradictory; and this very fact has ever been, and now is, the greatest wonder to the believer in spiritualism. For instance, in Chicago the spirit of some great general or statesman has reported himself present in the *seance;* and, after receiving the welcome of the circle, he has proceeded to deliver messages. But, strangely enough, the same noted character reports himself present, the very same moment, in some dark, curtained room in New York. And the same thing is repeated in New Orleans, and in San Francisco. The medium in each of those circles, in astonished wonder, receives the most wonderful intelligence from the spirit-world. But, alas for the veracity of the noted spirit, not one of his messages agrees with another! They are contradictory, and some of them senseless.

Then, they can not all be true. Who can explain this confusion? It is bungling, even for a devil.

Now, that noted spirits are often announced as present in different places, at the same time, will not be denied by any who are conversant with the "tricks of the trade." For this, indeed—as we have intimated—is to skilled spiritualists one of the most inexplicable feats in all spiritualism. A firm believer in the *seance* can never explain or understand it.

But, evidently, this is the solution, and the only reasonable one that can be given: There was no such spirit present in any one of those circles; but there were spirits of demons present, to answer the call of the several mediums in each of those distant cities. The medium chanced to call for the same spirit. Now, bear in mind, those demons are all the children of him who is the father of lies; and they do credit to their chief. So, when the medium, by certain cabalistic raps and signs known to the craft, asked if the spirit of Thomas Jefferson was present, the demons responded affirmatively. But these junior devils are finite, and not one could possibly know what the other was answering; hence the confusion and contradictions.

It is known to the world that, repeatedly, the spirits—which in all cases are demons, and not, as is supposed, the spirits of departed mortals—have been ensnared and confounded by unbelievers, who have asked them if the spirit of some distant but living friend was present. The spirit of the demon—as we have said—being finite, does not always know whether such person is dead or alive. And because the question is asked, he supposes the person dead, and readily personates him. All know that, by this means, astonished mediums have been made ashamed of the confusion.

But those demons have vast knowledge of, and acquaintance with, both men and things on the earth; and have thus been enabled to amaze and astonish the world, by reporting themselves to the spiritual medium as the spirit of some one not known to be dead. Inquiry has shown the man to have died without the knowledge of his friends at home. But the demon who personated him knew it; and that was a grand achievement for this heresy of Satan, spiritualism.

But, finally, we wish to conclude. Already we have extended our hunt after this dangerous heresy far beyond our original purpose. Our one purpose has been to save the honestly deceived—and they are many, for it is a dangerous snare—and to convince the confirmed spiritualist of the diabolism of his heresy. And this we think we have plainly proved, by common facts, by reason, and by the inspired Scriptures.

And now, with an earnest prayer to the God of all truth for your deliverance from this snare of Satan, we entreat you, "Believe not every spirit, but try the spirits whether they be of God." And may the great Eternal Spirit guide both you and us into the way of all wisdom and truth, and bring us at last into the safe abode of the spirits of the just, where we shall be forever content to abide in the presence of Jesus, by whose merit we are saved!

But, dear reader, while we have taken the ground—and, we think, fairly maintained it—that spiritualism is a snare of demons, by which they deceive poor bewildered mortals, by personating, in the *seance*, the friend whose spirit you call for, and that no such spirit of departed friend ever did or can answer your call, yet we allow the ministration of spirits, even to mortals on earth; and this we shall show in the following chapter on Bible Spiritualism.

IX.

BIBLE SPIRITUALISM; OR, THE MINISTRATION OF THE SPIRITS.

"Are they not all ministering spirits, sent forth to minister for them who shall be heirs of salvation?"—HEB. I, 14.

THE apostle, in this chapter, represents to the Hebrews the great favor of God in giving his Son to be the all-sufficient sacrifice for all. And to show his great superiority over all others, he presents him as a divine, or as an uncreated Savior, bringing messages of salvation unto them. There had been, from the beginning of the first promise of hope to man, messengers sent from God, with instruction and the encouragement of hope; but these were created beings, who only came to the heirs of salvation as instructed by the Master. Hence, they were but fellow-heirs or fellow-servants of the same God; but the superiority of Jesus is shown in that he possesses Divine Sonship, or is the uncreated Messenger of God to man. Our business with the subject now, is to ascertain the office, mission, and extent of the ministration of the spiritual messengers God is pleased to send into the world, and to what extent Christians are dependent upon them. We notice:

1. The meaning of ministering spirits.

The term spirit may, in this Scriptural sense, be defined as an immaterial, intelligent substance, or an immaterial, intelligent being.

Ministration signifies the act of performing service.

Ministering spirits, then, are messengers sent from God on some service.

The lesson also teaches the service rendered. But spirit, as applied to man, signifies the reasonable soul, which continues in being after the death of the body — the spiritual, reasoning, and choosing substance, capable of eternal happiness—and means the soul. Thus, when the dying Stephen said, in his last prayer on earth, "Lord Jesus, receive my spirit!" the prayer was for the reception of the soul by the Lord Jesus. The likeness and affinity is thus apparent. Intelligent souls, or the unembodied angels of God in heaven, and the embodied souls of the heirs of salvation on earth, each and all are the servants of the most high God.

The angels have kept their first estate, and their happiness is complete in the unclouded presence of their maker, God, and their immaterial wants are all met by his unobstructed hand; for in his presence there is fullness of joy, and at his right-hand there are pleasures for evermore.

But man is the victim of the Fall; and, though redeemed by the blood of Christ, yet he is still on trial; and, because of his weakness and imbecility of mind, he is likely to fail; for Satan is yet a tempting devil, bent on man's ruin. God would save him, and calls out to him, "Look unto me, all ye ends of the earth, and be ye saved." But poor man, in his blindness, shouts back, in his grief, "O, that I knew where I might find him!" To his plaintive wail of trouble God answers, "As I live, I have no pleasure in the death of him that dieth, but would rather all would turn unto me and live." "Turn ye, turn ye; for why will ye die?" The bewildered soul again calls out, while the bitterness of death is upon him, How shall I come? To his cry the voice of God's Word responds, "Let the wicked man forsake his ways and the unrighteous man his thoughts," and let him "repent and be converted;" for "except ye repent, ye shall all likewise perish." The sorrowing one, thus taught, exclaims, "I do repent; God be merciful to me a sinner!" and instantly there is joy in the presence of the angels of God; for angels ever manifest a lively interest in all that pertains to the glory of God and the salvation of man. Do you ask how the angels know? We answer, the truth is plainly taught in the Scriptures that these happy spirits have great knowledge of all that pertains to man on earth. What the medium of communication is, it must be confessed, is more a matter of conjecture. When the Scriptures would reduce it to our conception, figures of speech, suited to the knowledge of mortals, are used.

Thus, in Jacob's dream, a ladder seemed to rest on the earth, but its top touched the stepping-stone of the grand gateway of heaven, and the angels of God both ascended and descended; and the Savior told Nathaniel that he should see heaven open, and the angels of God ascending and descending upon the Son of Man. But both their descent to earth and ascent to heaven is in the interest of man, and is for the glory of God; for, "Are they not all ministering spirits, sent forth to minister for them who shall be heirs of salvation." And now we notice:

2. Their office and work with Christians.

The great apostle to the Gentiles charges Timothy to act a faithful part, "before God, and the Lord Jesus Christ, and the elect angels;" which, to our mind, plainly implies that he was all the time under their eye and inspection. The first preachers of the Gospel of Christ were not only the "gazing-stock of the earth," but were "a spectacle to angels."

How often or how constantly they accompany our footsteps, or what the medium of locomotion, is not now a question of importance; nor need we be curious to know why God—who knows us altogether, and has all power to help us—employs them for our comfort. We may not know; but may we not say: There are seasons when these sons of God speed on the wings of light from the eternal throne, charged with a mission of love, and freighted with the blessing of God, to some poor earth-worm, burdened with sorrow and care, lifting the burden, and cheering the heart? for "we have not a high-priest who can not be touched with the feelings of our infirmities, but was in all points tempted as we are, yet without sin, and angels came and ministered unto him," and he is, to the Christian, elder brother. Not only so, but with him the Christian is joint-heir.

If angels ministered unto Jesus, in his sore trial, and Christians are joint-heirs to the inheritance, might we not, without proof-texts, assume they delight to wait on and cheer the heart and hand of the weary pilgrim, as he sojourns in this wilderness of sin? But the proof is not lacking; for, "are they not all ministering spirits, sent to minister for them who shall be heirs of salvation?" How they do this, and to what extent, must be apparent from a few considerations; for we must bear in mind they are not cumbered with material bodies; hence, no estimate of the velocity of their movements can be made. And if it be true that matter offers no more resistance to spirit than to thought, then those spirits, messengers of God, may be kneeling at the throne eternal one moment of man's count, and, having received a message from God the Father, the next moment the messenger is cheering thy heart.

Let us think of it one moment. God is in heaven; his saints militant are on earth.

Now, God's children are as darling to him as the apple of an eye; but those children are, while on earth, exposed to the tempter's snare. They are also yet in school, and have much to learn; often their wisdom is at fault, and their ignorance leads them astray. Sometimes they are in doubt, and know not what is right. Paul says, "For we know not what we should pray for as we ought." But God sees it all, and God knows it all. The poor bewildered soul is bowed down and sorrowing; earth seems cold, dark, and dreary; and Satan tempts us with the thought: God has forgotten; "curse God and die." So he tempted Job; so he will tempt you. But, go back, ye gates of heaven, and let the eye of faith penetrate the inner glory! There, seated on the eternal throne, sits and reigns the omnipotent Father; at his side stands our High-priest, pleading for all his saints; before the throne, in countless throng, stand his saints, and the angels are all around. The Father hears and heeds; a messenger is called and counseled; then, freighted with love, speeds his flight to earth. He may go to the palace; he is sure to go to the cottage, where dwells the lone, sad-hearted widow, with words of cheer and the blessing of peace; for they minister to the heirs of salvation.

Are we asked why, and how? To the first we answer: God, who can speak a world from nought, and can do all things without an agency, chooses to carry on all his work by the use of means, and has, from the beginning, stamped both man and angel with nobility, by making them his acknowledged partners, especially in the great work of salvation. See Psalm ciii, 21 : "Bless ye the Lord, all ye his hosts; ye ministers of his, that do his pleasure." And also 2 Corinthians vi, 1 : "We then, as workers together with him, beseech you also that ye receive not the grace of God in vain;" or 2 Corinthians v, 20: "Now then we are ambassadors for Christ, as though God did beseech you by us: we pray you in Christ's stead, be ye reconciled to God."

By these Scriptures, the co-operation of both men and angels with God in his work is plainly taught. But the question is not of the fact, but the reason; and this is twofold: the glory of God and the ennobling and lifting up of the creature. For it must be borne in mind that, though all Christians are the servants of God, yet they are more—even partners with God in the great work of salvation. But as man works with God for the good of his fellow-man, so do the angels work for God, in helping man. We have already said the angels have a great knowledge of the affairs of men on the earth. We now advance to the thought of their great interest in those affairs. See 1 Peter i, 12: "Unto whom it was revealed, that not unto themselves, but unto us they did minister the things, which are now reported unto you by them that have preached the Gospel unto you with the Holy Ghost sent down from heaven; which things the angels desire to look into."

From this Scripture, and others, it is evident that angels are intensely interested in the work of our salvation, ever using their holy influence to win us to the way of life; and the proof is not wanting that they are sometimes commissioned to hedge us in, and prevent us from going into the paths of sin. The case of the false prophet is in point. Balak, King of the Moabites, seeing that Israel was much too strong for him, conceived the thought of getting Israel cursed by their God. There was none that could bring this about, in his judgment, save the prophet Balaam. Alas! he was wont to pronounce blessings on Israel.

But Balak sought him out, and said, "Curse me this people, for they are too mighty for me." The prophet treated the servants kindly; and, after counsel with God, he said to Balak's messengers, "Get you into your land, for the Lord refuseth to give me leave to go with you." When this word was brought to Balak, he was evidently sorely troubled, and he determined to send more honorable men, even princes. These said, "Let nothing hinder thee from coming to Balak; for he will promote thee unto very great honor, and will do whatsoever thou sayest; only curse Israel." Balaam was tempted; but had not yet determined to go contrary to the word of the Lord—no, not even for a "house full of gold and silver;" but God, after having plainly shown him that he did not approve of his going, gave him permission. Balaam hurried to seize the reward of iniquity; and would have cursed Israel, but God sent his angel to stop up his way. How angry was Balaam when first hindered! how he smote the beast, whose eyes first beheld the angel! And not until his own eyes were opened to behold the heavenly visitant was he aware of his great sin in striving to curse Israel. And when he came to Balak, and the sacrifices were all prepared, he could only say, "How shall I curse whom God hath not cursed? or how shall I defy whom the Lord hath not defied?"

Here, then, is a plain case of the restraining influence of ministering spirits, sent from God to his servants on earth. Without it, in this case, the prophet must have fallen a victim to the snare of his tempter.

May we not infer his children of to-day are equally the objects of his care?

Saul of Tarsus thought he was doing God service when he persecuted the believers in Jesus; but God's Holy Spirit arrested him in his course of madness, and directed him in the way of life.

But those heavenly messengers not only serve as guardian shields to his saints on earth, but they also serve as counselors and comforters of all who seek the fellowship of God. "I will not leave you comfortless," said Jesus; "I will come unto you;" and on the inauguration-day of Christianity, or the day of Pentecost, the Holy Ghost, in comforting power, fell on the believers in Jesus.

Then Paul and Silas, in the prison, witnessed the presence and felt the power of the heavenly apparition. So did Peter, though in the gloomy jail; and, to his inexpressible joy, his chains fell off, and he was free from the loathsome dungeon. But we are all concerned to know whether such heavenly visitants are composed of the Holy Spirit of God and the angels of heaven, or do the spirits of the dead in Christ ever revisit the earth?

Bishop D. W. Clark, in his "Man all Immortal," page 206, says:

"Among those myriads of angelic messengers, is it not possible that there should sometimes be found one who was once an inhabitant of earth? Is it not possible that our departed kindred, our parents, our companions, our dear children, that passed from us in the bloom of life, a loved brother or sister, may revisit earth and come to minister to us in that which is holy and good; to breathe around us influences that will draw us heavenward? If it be possible to revisit earth, this, no doubt, is the glorious mission on which they would desire to come.

"The form in which the spirit of the departed might be expected to visit us, would be that of spiritual communion. There are seasons when the soul seems to recognize the presence of, and to hold communion with, the departed. They are like angelic visitants: we meet them in our lonely walks, in our deep and solemn meditations, and in our closet communings; we meet them when the lengthening shadows hallow the eventide—mysterious and solemn is their communion; we meet them when sorrows encompass us round about, and hallowed is the influence their presence imparts. Who shall say that at such times there is not a real communion between the living and the dead?"

Hannah More, when dying, extended her arms as if to embrace some one, called the name of a beloved sister, long before departed, and exclaimed "Joy!" and expired. Hosts of similar cases might be given, in which dying saints have given evidence of the presence of loved ones, long in the spirit-land; but we forbear, that we may notice:

3. The goodness of God in such wise provision.

The desire for immortality is found to

exist in the heart of all intelligent beings, and it is scarcely possible for the mind to conceive of a more revolting thing than annihilation.

Spiritualists of modern days make stronger claim of immortality from spirit revelations than from the Bible; indeed, some assert that spiritualism must be maintained or immortality must be denied. To this we dissent; for the interpretation given of spiritualism, by spiritualists, is just as opposite to the ministration of spirits as light from darkness, or righteousness from sin. But, thank God! we are not left to grope our way in the dark uncertainties of spiritual *seance* for the blessed assurance of immortality and eternal life; but God's blessed Word thrills with the breathings of the spirit-life on almost every page; and, to assure comfort, and encourage our holy longings, he gives first his Spirit, as a reminder and as a comforter. And this is but in accordance with the promise of the

Lord Jesus, "Lo, I am with you alway, even to the end of the world."

The Christian, pleading this immortality pledge, realizes the truth of that sublime exclamation of the Christian poet:

> "My God is reconciled,
> His pardoning voice I hear;
> He owns me for his child,
> I can no longer fear.
> His Spirit answers to the blood,
> And tells me I am born of God."

With such blessed assurance of an immortal heirship with Jesus, can the proof of my immortality be wanting? Nay: but I grasp the Bible truth, "Because he [that is, Christ] liveth, I shall live also."

And such blessed assurance is given by his Word and by his Spirit; and to it all the saints on earth and in heaven stand witness.

Who cheered the heart of the dying M'Kendree, as, in the final struggle, he exclaimed, "All is well?"

Multiplied thousands of such cases could be given, all showing the presence of ministering spirits, who have accompanied the saint in life; and, in the parting hour, the heavenly watchers stand ready to waft the astonished saint to their heavenly bowers.

Christian pilgrim, were you ever thrown into a new circle of society, where you looked for strangers? What was your astonishment and joy, to find yourself in the midst of warmest friends! The itinerant minister will feel the force of this; for this experience has thrilled his heart often in life, as he and his family have gone up and down in the earth, preaching Christ and the great salvation, with no home but the hearts of his people.

Ah! we shall not be strangers in heaven, nor embarrassed for company; for some one of the ministering spirits, who have ministered to us in life, will stand ready to introduce us, and to show us round the great city; and all our friends, relatives, and acquaintances will greet us on the eternal shore. Shall we know them? O yes: we knew them in life; we saw them in death, and were not deceived; and now they meet us at the dividing line.

"My father and the chariots!" has thrilled the hearts of thousands in all ages; and you and I may be permitted to exclaim, erelong, as our ransomed spirits are freed from these earth-clogs, "My father, my mother, my child, my son or my daughter, my Savior! for, 'are they not all ministering spirits, sent forth to minister for them who shall be the heirs of salvation?'" Amen.

X.

SPIRITUALISM A LOVER OF DARKNESS.

"And this is the condemnation, that light is come into the world, and men loved darkness rather than light, because their deeds were evil."—JOHN III, 19.

SINCE the introduction of sin into the world, a characteristic feature of the sinner's deeds has been a love of darkness and a hatred of the light. And so deep-seated is this in the hearts of men, that even when moved to deeds of righteousness, in their first inception, they seek the privacy or cover of darkness. He to whom the above quotation was addressed was doubtless convinced that Jesus was a teacher sent from God, and was persuaded that he could tell him about the way of life. Hence, he was moved to go to Jesus for instruction; but, for some reason, went at night. During the conversation that followed, Jesus called his attention to this love of darkness by the unregenerate. "They love darkness rather than light, because their deeds are evil."

"Light has come into the world."

"Let there be light," was the exclamation of Jehovah, which dispersed the gloom and drove back the long chaotic night of the ages. Light is of Divine origin. "And God saw the light that it was good, and he divided it from the darkness, calling it day; but he called the darkness night."

In Scripture parlance, all that is good, pure, and true is called light; while all that is vile and impure is called darkness—sometimes blackness. And this is truly characteristic of righteousness and sin. Man was originally a creature of the light, and the redeemed are always called children of the light. It is only while men are rejecting salvation that they love the darkness and hate the light.

Scientists attempt to define the properties of light, and to detect its origin. Thus, we have the theory of emanation, which supposes light to be a material fluid, of extreme subtlety, emanating in particles from a luminous body. Then we have the theory of undulation, asserting that light is produced by the undulations of an independent medium, set in motion by some luminous body, losing sight of the fact there can be no luminous body without light.

Now, all this but puzzles the brain of the student; and by such scientific rules he will hardly determine whether the natural light is an emanation of the sun, the most luminous body, or whether the sun is the reflex concentration of the light. But this we know, God commanded the existence of light; and, seeing the light, he pronounced it good, and divided it from the darkness.

After this, he commanded lights for the firmament of the heaven: the greater one, the sun, to rule the day; the lesser ones, the moon and the stars, to rule the night.

Skeptics and infidels reject this Bible account of the origin and existence of light before the existence or construction of the sun. But this class of maudlin thinkers reject all that the Bible records of God and of God's works, simply because their finite minds can not grasp infinity. The Christian, seeing these in hopeless confusion—for they do not themselves agree—turns boldly to the Scriptural truth, whether the light is dealt out to mortal gaze by the sun, moon, or stars.

God is the author of it; for he commanded it into being before any of these concentrated bodies of it were hung up in the heavens for the gaze of earth's inhabitants. Deity is the embodiment of light, and in him there is no darkness at all.

But it follows, if God is light, then they that are his walk in the light. David meant this when he said, "They shall walk, O Lord, in the light of thy countenance: they shall still be praising thee."

But again: light is but an emanation of Deity; and, if so, then where God dwells there must be an infinite day. Earth is but his footstool; but heaven is his dwelling-place. When John, in Apocalyptic gaze, peered over the embattled walls of heaven, he exclaimed, with rapture: "There is no night there;" for "the Lord God Almighty and the Lamb are the temple of it." "And the city had no need of the sun, neither of the moon, to shine in it; for the glory of God did lighten it, and the Lamb is the light thereof."

God, then, is light; and the character of it must be purity and holiness. Friend, does it shine upon thy pathway? Then,

> "Walk in the light; so shalt thou know
> That fellowship of love
> His Spirit only can bestow,
> Who reigns in light above."

But what are the revelations of light?

1. It brings to our senses a knowledge of existent facts. The glories of earth and heaven are no better than the dungeon to the blind; for all is dark to them. In our humane asylums for the blind, the teachers accomplish much for the poor unfortunate inmates, making them, happily, not only masters in the cunning arts, but imparting to them also a knowledge of letters. Yet here is the limit of their power; and a knowledge of color, of the rainbow tints, and the beauties of nature, no teacher ever yet imparted to the born blind.

As in the physical, so in the moral world. The light of God never falls upon the eye of the alien soul. No infidel's creed ever yet brought a knowledge of the true God, or declared the revelations of Heaven. To such it is all mystery—all gloom; for the eye of their understanding is darkened. There is no light in them; and this is their condemnation: they love the darkness, and cherish the gloom.

But it is the province of the light, if permitted, to dispel the darkness and drive away the gloom; and this it does for all who will come into it. But here is the strangest anomaly: light has come into the world, but men reject it, cherishing the gloom. They continue to stumble into the dark pits of doubt and sin. God has graciously given his Word to shine as a lamp of life; but men reject it as all dark and full of mystery. The good Spirit of God has been given to enlighten the world; but men resist the strivings of the Spirit and grieve it away, while they remain in the darkness of nature's night.

It needs no argument to convince men of the truth of some unsupplied want of their nature; for there is, evidently, at least a partial knowledge of something wrong, of possible danger, which leaves men restless and unsettled. Nothing can be more apparent than the truth of the Scriptural declaration, "There is no peace to the wicked." In evidence, study the teeming millions of our race who reject God and his Word, as they struggle in hopeless unrest. See them in heathen lands, as they grope in the dark. See them in Christian lands, as they fly to every refuge of lies, in the vain hope of finding rest and quiet for the wretched conscience.

But we wish to offer one thought more of the light; and that is, its accessibility for all; and in this may be seen the goodness of God.

The greater light that rules the day—our sun—is, we maintain, the concentration, or the embodied form, of material light; and this is so centrally hung up in the firmament of heaven, that all the inhabitants of the earth may behold its rays and walk in its light. And under its warming influence, the great world of vegetation is quickened into life, joy, beauty, and gladness. "The Lord

God is a Sun and a Shield." The Lord Jesus is the Sun of Righteousness, and it pleased the Father that in him should all fullness dwell. This great light is for the lightening of the eyes of earth's blinded millions. Has he not declared that this was the great purpose of his being lifted up, that he might draw all men unto himself?

Men stumble in mines and pits, with but the flickering, artificial light of the taper, while the great blazing sun is shining with a perfect flood of light in the heavens above them. So, even in Christian lands, in the light of the Gospel of Christ, men stumble in the dark pits of sin, strangely—ah! stubbornly—shutting the eye of reason and faith against every ray of light, which, if admitted, must discover to them not only their folly, but also their danger, and the only way out of it. "This is their condemnation."

But "they love darkness." And this will lead us to speak of the character of darkness.

And as we have, in the forepart of this chapter, maintained that God is the embodiment and author of light, and attempted to show that all who are his walk in the light, so, now, we assert, and shall proceed to prove, that Satan is prince of darkness, and that all his servants stumble in the dark.

We are wont to speak of what we do not understand as dark, all dark, Satan has ever plied his hellish arts in the dark. So he came to the first pair; and, under the dark, impenetrable pall of false pretense, he accomplished his work of diabolism. He has never changed his cursed tactics; for they have been altogether too successful in deluding souls to ruin to be given up; and with mysterious, dark, and damning schemes, he entangles men to this day. Hence, he is truthfully called the prince of darkness, and the dark adversary.

This being his character, we are not surprised that his foulest deeds are wrought in darkness. We have given the case of Saul, King of Israel. While he remained a righteous man, he was wont to consult God in all that pertained to his kingdom. And this he did before the altars of God, in open day, through the prophets of the God of Israel. But when he—by his sins—had lost the favor of God, he sought not only impenetrable disguise, but the cover of a dark night, to confer with the witch of En-dor.

So, to-day, while men love mercy and deal justly, and worship the God of their fathers, they seek Heaven's broadest light; but when their deeds are evil, and they are without the light of the grace of God in their hearts, then do they seek the mantle of thick darkness; and, carefully excluding the light, they seek audience with the spirits of darkness. And here, in the dark, does the restless, God-forsaken heart of thousands in our day, in this Christian land, under the deceptive name of spiritualism, offer strange service at the altars of strange gods. Under the delusion that they are holding conference with the spirits of the dead, they blindly confer with demoniacal spirits; or, as Isaiah says, they confer with wizards that peep.

But so has Satan ever worked. His first efforts are to blind the eyes of the understanding; and such are his deceptive powers, that men under his influence imagine they see more clearly than all others. This makes the conflict between light and darkness all the greater; for, if men imagine they see, all the world can not make them believe they are in darkness.

Take, in proof, the bigoted Catholic, of this or any country. Taught by an unholy priesthood to believe in the power of the priest to grant special indulgence, the deluded devotee will go straightway from solemn mass to the beer-garden or brothel, where, in riotous sin, debauchery, and shame, he will spend God's most holy day, under the delusive conviction that he has permission to do so, because he has paid his money to "father confessor in Holy Mother Church."

Are you shocked at this, pious Protestant? Well, know this: you can no more change him from his convictions, that he has a perfect right thus to indulge in beastly lusts, than you can change the laws of gravity; for so he is taught from his infancy. Satan has deluded the priest, and the priest has deluded the man; and thus a chain of deceptions—well-connected—has run from Pope to laity for many generations. Gross darkness has, indeed, covered the people.

Now, it is evident to the thinking that this accursed, ruinous system has been, and now is, kept up and perpetuated by deception. And the deception is preserved and sustained by withholding the Bible from the hands of the common members of this "mother of harlots." Or, in other words, give the Bible to the members of the Catholic Church, and in ten years it would either be reformed or it would pass out of existence.

But we have said it is Satan's policy to delude and keep men in the dark. His banner is the mantle of thick darkness. Under this, he matures his plans for the ruin of souls; and he even laughs at the light of heaven or the revelation of God's Word, so long as he can hold men under the folds of his flag, which is darkness and doubt.

Of course, there is much confusion in the ranks of his votaries, because they are in the dark; and it would not be reasonable to expect them even to understand themselves, much less one another. Consequently, we find in Satan's service a conglomerate mass, agreeing in but one thing; namely, they all "love darkness, because their deeds are evil." Some are openly infidel, some are atheists, some are Universalists, some are free-lovers, some are freethinkers, and many are spiritualists; but, as admitted, all love darkness, and are opposed to God and righteousness. And all are in restless confusion, and are like blind men groping their way in the dark; and are ready to follow after every *ignis-fatuus* of demoniacal or human device. But such is the character of darkness, to confuse and to confound.

Nor is it strange that no single faction of Satan's votaries agree among themselves. Perhaps the fairest sample of this is found among spiritualists. That some of them are advocates of good morals and decency, cherishing some respect for chastity and virtue, will not be denied. But what Christian father or mother, or what man or woman who has one grain of respect for virtue, could read the reports of their late convention—held in Cincinnati—without the tinge of shame mantling the brow. And yet the reports went into thousands of Christian families, to the insult of decency and the disgrace of public journalism.

One blatant shrew (a Miss B.), in a speech at the above convention, defied any man in the convention to tell which of the children of the household were his own. And it must be told, to the everlasting disgrace of this convention of spiritualists, that this flippant, insulting, defiant challenge was loudly cheered.

Tell it not to the heathen of any land where we have Christian missionaries, but these are the people who claim to have taken advanced ground in spiritual knowledge!

But stay, reader. Do n't suppose, from the seeming openness of the above speech, and the daylight sessions of the conventions this people hold throughout the country, that they are therefore not afraid of the light. Nay: these are but the external outcroppings of the damning lessons studied in the dark *seance*, where demons are the tutors, and lecherous men and women are the students. Here, in this school of Satan, lessons are learned fit only for the brothel, and corrupting enough to ruin a saint—lessons at once an outrage upon humanity and contradictory of all God's Word; but these lessons are all learned in the dark, and are as secret as the Roman confessional.

Some respectable spiritualists—for such there are, despite the corrupting influences to which they are exposed by association—will think these strictures lacking in charity; but such unfortunate persons as have fallen victims to this Satanic agency will need no proof that the vilest and most corrupt men and women of this age, both in Europe and America, are most prominent in the *seance*, or so-called spiritual circle. And here, with every ray of light shut out, these vile, brutish demons incarnate come into closest contact with the husbands, wives, and daughters of respectable families, and sometimes—it may be—with virtuous young men and women. How long virtue could be maintained with such associations, is a question many have solved to their shame and sorrow, having proved by sad experience that "evil communications corrupt good manners."

But already we have extended this chapter beyond what we intended. We close it with the Scriptural warning: "This is the condemnation, that light is come into the world; and men loved darkness rather than light, because their deeds were evil."

THE END.

www.ingramcontent.com/pod-product-compliance
Lightning Source LLC
Chambersburg PA
CBHW021729220426
43662CB00008B/772